THE POLITICS OF
GREEK TRAGEDY

This introductory guide uses close examination of specific plays to demonstrate to a student and general audience how and why Greek tragedy should be read as a political art form. It is an important topic and one that has been given a brief and selective treatment in recent general accounts of Greek tragedy.

The book sets the plays in the historical context of the fifth-century Greek city-state and shows how – like the contemporary satirical comedy of Aristophanes, or indeed the sculptures of the Parthenon – tragedy had a highly political dimension.

After a general survey of the political aspects of Athenian tragedy, the author goes on to provide stimulating in-depth analyses of Sophocles' *Ajax* and *Antigone* and Euripides' *Suppliants* and *Trojan Women*. The final chapter, on the 'reception' of political tragedy, looks at some theatre, film and TV productions of these plays that have taken an overtly political stance within their modern context.

D.M. Carter was Head of Classics at Watford Grammar School for Boys and is now Lecturer in Greek at the University of Reading. He is the author of several articles on Greek tragedy and Greek political thought.

GREECE AND ROME LIVE

Also available in this series:

Forthcoming titles:

THE POLITICS

OF

GREEK TRAGEDY

D. M. Carter

BRISTOL
PHOENIX
PRESS

Cover illustration: *Electra at the Tomb of Agamemnon* (oil on canvas) by Leighton, Frederic (1830–96); © Ferens Art Gallery, Hull City Museums and Art Galleries/ The Bridgeman Art Library

First published in 2007 by
Bristol Phoenix Press
an imprint of The Exeter Press
Reed Hall, Streatham Drive
Exeter, Devon EX4 4QR
UK
www.exeterpress.co.uk

British Library Cataloguing in Publication Data
A catalogue record for this book is available from the British Library

Paperback ISBN 13: 978 1 904675 16 7
Hardback   ISBN 13: 978 1 904675 50 1

Typeset by Carnegie Book Production, Lancaster in Chaparral Pro 11pt on 15pt
Printed in Great Britain by Antony Rowe Ltd, Chippenham

For Alice

CONTENTS

PREFACE

R ecent years have seen heightened interest in Greek tragedy as a political medium, both on the ancient and the modern stage. I hesitate to add to the already groaning weight on the shelves that support writing on this topic; however, I hope that three aspects of this book will be distinctive. The first is to get across an idea of why modern scholarship finds this topic so exciting. The city that from the late sixth century BC gave the world democracy was at exactly the same time developing tragic drama; it seems that any study to make a connection between the two will strike at the heart of Athenian culture. This (alongside the evidence of the plays) might explain the continued interest of classicists in the political function of tragedy. But secondly, I am not looking here for a single, unifying theory. The weakness of some approaches has been the attempt to build a universal model of a political tragedy, often in terms of some other aspect of ancient Greek culture: a historical event, a type of ritual, or (most often) democracy itself. Such rules will always be broken by the many available exceptions. That said, the tragedies do for the most part share an underlying set of political values, which I explore in ch. 3. Thirdly, it will not do merely to *assume* that performances on the tragic stage were political. Some space will be devoted, therefore, to explaining why these plays are considered political, and indeed what we mean by 'political'.

A brief word on the order of the chapters. Chapter 1 makes some methodological points and supplies necessary background information on the Greek city-state and Greek tragedy. Chapter 2 is a survey of modern views, which raises and explores many of the most important issues in this book. Chapter 3 presents my own ideas. Some readers may feel that they are kept waiting too long for the right answer; if so it is possible to read Chapter 3 first and refer back to Chapter 2. Chapter 4 is a discussion of four political tragedies, while Chapter 5 looks briefly at the political impact of tragedy in modern performance. The comparisons offered in this last chapter set up some conclusions.

This book assumes no knowledge of ancient Greek and no prior knowledge of the plays. However, the reader will get the most out of this book by reading the following plays first: Aeschylus' Oresteian trilogy (comprising *Agamemnon*, *Libation Bearers* and *Eumenides*), Sophocles' *Ajax* and *Antigone*, and Euripides' *Suppliants* and *Trojan Women*. This book is therefore designed for the student and the general reader; but I hope it is also interesting to professionals in the field, specifically in the ways in which it offers to move the current debate forwards. Above all, I aim to explore ways in which the concerns of the classical Greek *polis*, taken as a general category, are mapped onto the dramas.

I have aimed as far as possible for consistency in the spelling of Greek words and names. Broadly, one can either transliterate the Greek letters (writing, for example, about 'the *khoros* in Sophokles' *Trakhiniai*') or one can Latinise ('the chorus in Sophocles' *Trachiniae*'). Either system is correct and it is difficult to stick to one system to the complete exclusion of the other. I tend to Latinise proper nouns and transliterate other Greek words. I quote faithfully on a few occasions from modern authors who prefer to transliterate Greek names. Greek plays are referred to by their English titles; so, for example, *Trachiniae* becomes *Women of Trachis*. Readers should be aware that Sophocles' *Oedipus the King* is commonly referred to by classicists as *Oedipus Tyrannus* or simply *OT*; it is also, of course, known as

Oedipus Rex. Aeschylus' *Libation Bearers* is frequently published under the Latinised Greek title: *Choephori*. Other alternative titles can be found in Appendix B.

The titles of plays can give rise to one other source of confusion. It may help readers who are new to the subject to know that there are two surviving tragedies called *Electra*, one by Sophocles and the other by Euripides; they in very different ways dramatise the killing of Clytemnestra by her son Orestes, the subject also of Aeschylus' *Libation Bearers*. There are also two extant plays called *Suppliants*, by Aeschylus and Euripides, which tell completely separate stories from each other. I discuss the former in Chapters 2 and 3, and the latter in Chapter 4.

Most of the translations from tragedy in this book are taken from the complete series of Greek tragedies edited by David Grene and Richmond Lattimore (Chicago University Press). The passages from Aeschylus' *Suppliants* on pages 86–7 come from the Penguin Classics edition by Philip Vellacott. The translations from Sophocles' *Ajax* on pages 95 and 97, and the translation from Euripides' *Ion* on page 72, are my own. I am also responsible for translations from Aristophanes and the Old Oligarch. All other translations from Greek texts come from the Penguin Classics series. For quotation from Bertolt Brecht's *Antigone des Sophokles* I have used the translation by Judith Malina (New York, 1984).

My thanks go firstly and most importantly to John Betts, whose idea this book was. Sadly, illness has prevented him from seeing the project through as editor, and I am very grateful to Anna Henderson of The Exeter Press for all her help in the final stages. Much of the research for Chapter 5 was conducted in Oxford at the Archive of Performances of Greek and Roman Drama. Anthony Podlecki read and commented on the whole manuscript and answered several further queries beyond the call of duty. Alan Sommerstein read drafts of several chapters and was characteristically generous with his comments. I also benefited from the advice of Alastair Blanshard, Barbara Goff, Amy Smith and Amanda Wrigley on individual chapters. Alice Carter and Awena Carter helped me with my prose style, and Tom Payne with verse translations. The index was prepared by Zeb Korycinska. None of these readers should be held responsible for any errors in this book, and the views expressed remain my own.

CHAPTER 1

INTRODUCTION

How can tragedy be political?

Early in the year 405 BC (by the modern calendar) the Athenians were facing defeat and possible annihilation at the hands of Sparta. Nearly thirty years of on-off conflict were heading for a disastrous end. At this moment of political crisis they did what they always did, twice a year, and held a dramatic festival. One of the plays performed, a comedy by Aristophanes called *Frogs*, addressed the city's problems in a way that might seem surprising to a modern audience. As the action starts the god Dionysus (in whose honour the dramatic festivals were held) is on his way to the underworld. He says he is going there to bring back his favourite writer of tragedies, Euripides, who had died the year before. On arrival in Hades he finds that Euripides has challenged Aeschylus (a tragedian from a previous generation) for the honours given to the best tragic poet among the dead. Dionysus is asked to judge between them and, after a long debate, Aeschylus wins. Dionysus then reveals his real – extraordinary – reason for coming to the underworld: he wants to find a poet to save the city. In a finale full of hope and expectation of some kind, he leads Aeschylus back to Athens from the dead.

Frogs is a fascinating and important drama for several reasons. It is a comic masterpiece of slapstick, innuendo and absurdism. It also lampoons the tragedies of Aeschylus and Euripides at some length: the result is effectively the earliest developed piece of

European literary criticism. The arguments given by the ghosts of Aeschylus and Euripides over what makes good and bad poetry are designed primarily to raise a laugh, but the laughs are clearly meant to come from an audience that knew its tragedy well and appreciated it. Knowing remarks are made about characterisation, narrative and metre, but most of all about the social and political importance of tragedy. Consider the following dialogue between the two dead poets (lines 1052–6). Here, Euripides defends his decision to dramatise the story of Phaedra in two separate plays called *Hippolytus*. The text of the second, rather less scandalous version has survived: in this play Phaedra is in love with her stepson Hippolytus; she tries to keep her feelings secret but, when Hippolytus finds out, kills herself having left a note that accuses him falsely of rape. In the earlier version it seems that Phaedra was more the proactive temptress.[1]

EURIPIDES: And did I tell the tale of Phaedra wrongly?
AESCHYLUS: God, no – it was correct. But nonetheless
    A poet ought to hide the wicked thing,
    Ought *not* to introduce or teach it. For,
    Whereas there is a teacher to advise
    Among the boys, the grown-ups have their poets.
    So much the more must we relate what's decent.

That the poet is a teacher was a popular idea in ancient Greece and the only one on which the Aristophanic Aeschylus and Euripides agree. Compare lines 1009–10:

AESCHYLUS: Tell me, for what must one admire a poet?
EURIPIDES: For cleverness and ready warning, since
    We make the people better in their cities.

What did the poet teach? The answer, in *Frogs*, is citizenship. It is on the nature of this education that Aristophanes sets the two dead poets against each other. The older poet believes that a poet should teach traditional values by providing heroic examples for the citizens to follow; the younger one says that tragedy should prompt its audience to question these values. One can compare two debates that still feature today in TV and radio discussion programmes and on the letters pages of newspapers. The first is about education: should we be training children to be good, or should we encourage them to think for themselves? The second concerns censorship in drama: do the writers of plays and TV shows have a duty to reflect everything that goes in modern life or to be more uplifting? (Does violence on TV encourage violence in society or provide an honest reflection of it?) I should add that Aristophanes is presenting caricatures of poets; the values that lie behind their respective dramas are more subtle and less sharply differentiated than this, as I hope will become apparent in this book.

To say that poetry could save a city from defeat seems patently ridiculous; but behind the comic idea is a serious point, which I think was felt by many Athenians at the time. It was not long after they lost the war that they began to look around for scapegoats. In 399 BC the philosopher Socrates was executed for believing in the wrong gods and for corrupting the Athenian young. An implication was that the moral fibre of the most recent generation of Athenian fighting men had been worn away. *Frogs* seems designed to please people who could make similar accusations against Euripides. In reality the Athenians lost the war because they depended on imported grain; when the Spartans, with Persian help, were finally able to defeat Athens at sea, the supply was cut off. Nevertheless, the idea that the warlike spirit of the Athenians had been dulled might have appealed to the popular imagination on the following grounds: the poet had a responsibility to provide good examples for the citizens; Euripides' tendency to question political values was damaging to morale; contrast Aeschylus, who came from Athens' golden age and had himself fought the Persians at Marathon. It is easy to see how the Athenians invested their poets with a certain responsibility. In other words, while it stretches the imagination to say that good poetry could save the city, it was arguable that 'bad' poetry could destroy it.

When we talk about political drama we probably mean one of two things. Either we mean drama in which the main players are political figures: plays about kings and princes, presidents and parliamentarians. Or we mean drama that is meant to have a political function in society. We might refer to these as, respectively, the 'weaker' and 'stronger' senses of the political in drama. Almost all Greek tragedy is political in the weaker sense, given that nearly every surviving play features at least one character who holds political office as the king of a city. But when modern commentators refer to Greek tragedy as political drama, they tend to mean the stronger idea. The whole of this book supports the view that Greek tragedy can be political in the weaker sense. Much of it argues for the stronger sense also, making the following two points in particular (both of which have been made in various ways before): tragedy could engage with contemporary issues and (occasionally) events; and the festival at which the plays were performed can be considered as a political organ, allowing the audience to reflect on issues and problems relevant to city life.

Against this view it can be said that the political function of tragedy has been overstated; that 'poetics' matter more than 'politics'.[2] This objection is based on the reasonable view that the primary function of drama is not to change society but to entertain the audience. Although this book does not really engage with this argument, I shall address it very briefly now. I have no intention of denying that a tragedy is designed to entertain in the sense that it provokes what Aristotle calls the peculiar pleasures of tragedy: feelings of pity and fear in those that watch it (Aristotle, *Poetics* 1453b1–13). However, most (not all) tragedies have some political function alongside the poetic one. Any book on Greek tragedy must concentrate on some aspects at the expense of others; this book demonstrates that Greek tragedy had an undeniable political importance.

The evidence of Aristophanes' *Frogs* indicates that the Greeks themselves understood tragedy to be political in the stronger sense: they expected tragedy to perform a function in the city. However, tragedy does not restrict its politics to the Aristophanic idea of an education in citizenship. Political tragedies (in the weaker sense) are concerned not only with relations between citizens; they can also dramatise the interaction of a citizen with the wider community, with political authority and with the law. (Note, by the way, that in Greek political thought the citizen is every bit as important a political player as those kings and presidents I mentioned before.) The role of cities can also be of interest: both in governing and protecting the lives of its citizens; and in dealing with enemies, suppliants (seekers of political asylum, in this context) and other foreigners.

Two methodological principles underpin this book. First, if we are to discuss political aspects of tragedy, we must be clear about what we mean by 'political'. If drama is to perform some function beyond entertainment, then we can think broadly about its *social* function: the ways in which events on stage relate to the real lives of audience members. To go one stage further and talk about the *political* function of tragedy, we must tease apart the specifically political from the merely social. This book devotes quite lot of space to this exercise, artificial though it admittedly is. If, however, we are in any doubt that the terms 'social' and 'political' are applicable to Greek tragedy, we should observe that these categories exist side-by-side in the plays: this is exemplified by the interaction between individuals, households and cities, and the ways in which these interactions are staged (see ch. 3).

The central character in this book – in some ways the central political player in Greek tragedy – is the Greek city-state, the *polis*. In the diversity of political dramas, and potential responses to them, it is often possible to pick out issues of special interest to democratic Athens, but (I shall argue) a study of tragic politics should maintain its focus on the city-state more generally. I therefore define the political for the purpose of this book as 'a concern with human beings as part of the community of the *polis*' (ch. 3; this is adapted from the definition given by C.W. Macleod, on whom see ch. 2).

As for the second point of method, it pays to bear in mind the audience for whom a poet intended these dramas at first perform- ance. Much of this book is concerned with what we might guess the original audience made of the plays; this might even be called an exercise in 'audience studies' (for a rationale, see further pages 26–7 below). Although occasionally we can identify the poet's own view with certainty, tragedy should also reveal political issues that were of interest to the audience and related to the political culture in which they lived. Some of these issues are not always the first that spring to mind: not just how to be a good citizen but whether one can claim citizenship at all; how a city should treat foreign suppliants; how to treat one's enemies once they have died. The first of these issues reflects the high value placed by the Greeks on citizen status; the second is used to reinforce an important aspect of Athenian political ideology;[3] the third reveals an area of Greek ethics on which there seems to have been no certain line. We shall see that tragedy as a genre is well equipped to raise tricky problems like this last issue. However (at the risk of making a clichéd point), more questions are asked in tragedy than answers given; certainly a tragic poet was less likely to pronounce on political issues than some prose writers were. Moreover, we cannot assume that the audience responded unanimously to the politics of the drama. The audience was not a single, homogeneous body but a uniquely varied collection of individuals from almost all over the Greek world, as we shall see later in this chapter.

This will lead me to reject the view of some modern writers, who explain the politics of tragedy in terms of mass, collective experience: in other words, that tragedy was a political art form because the citizens of Athens sat down together at the festival and this promoted cohesion in the city.[4] While it is undoubtedly true that shared entertainment promotes a clubbable sense of togetherness, I think the political significance of this can be overstated. The appreciation of tragic pleasures can be called a collective experience; the appreciation of political messages arguably cannot (on this point, see page 102 below). For this reason, and given the infrequency with which tragic poets make their own views clear, it is often hard to find the prescriptive agenda in tragedy that the Aristophanic Aeschylus prefers; for the most part the plays merely describe for us what may have been current concerns. Perhaps I can go further: sometimes the tragic poets create dramatic problems around these concerns, putting popular values to the test (this is certainly what is going on in Sophocles' *Antigone* – see ch. 4). The dramatic festivals therefore had no dynamic political role but instead provided a moment for political reflection: it is in this opportunity that we find tragedy to be political in the stronger sense.

Underlying nearly all the plays, however, is a constant political value: the importance of a strong and stable *polis*, the principal source of safety and security for its citizens. I shall demonstrate in ch. 3 that this idea is mapped onto the very staging of the plays. The different ways in which characters assert the importance of the city are put to the test in several plays (see ch. 4), but the values of the *polis* tend to emerge intact. This applies to any Greek city in tragedy, although Athens is portrayed as especially secure for its own citizens as well as for foreign suppliants. Tragic political values can therefore be described ultimately as establishment values, and not (as in much modern political theatre) part of the counter-culture.

Early Greek politics

In the rest of this chapter I want to supply some necessary background on ancient Greek politics and drama. Some readers may feel able to skip these introductory discussions.

The conduct of modern politics revolves around the idea of the nation state, an autonomous country with its own laws and government. The distinctive institution of ancient Greek politics was the *city*-state. Each city governed itself and the territory around it; citizenship meant membership of a city. The Greek word for city-state is *polis*. Our world 'politics' derives from the Greek *ta politika* – the affairs of the *polis*. There were hundreds of *poleis* in classical Greece, most with a population of no more than a few thousand people. A small number of cities had populations in the tens of thousands: these included Corinth and Thebes, yet the largest was Athens. Athens may have had a citizen body of 30,000 to 50,000 at its fifth-century peak; from these figures a total population can be extrapolated of between 150,000 and 300,000 people living in and around the city. This included an unusually large number of resident aliens, known as metics.[5]

The Greeks understood the stories of heroic myth to be their early history. This reflects a shared memory of cities that were ruled by kings, as was generally the case in Greece during the Mycenaean period. Given the size of some cities, many of these 'kings' would seem to a modern observer more like feudal chieftains. In Homer's *Odyssey*, Odysseus returns to the small island of Ithaca, of which he is king. Descriptions of his house make it sound large – over a hundred suitors are able to dine in his halls (Homer, *Odyssey* 16.247–54) – but hardly palatial. His son Telemachus, when he visits mighty

Sparta for the first time, is wonder-struck by the majesty of the court of king Menelaus (3.42–5). Odysseus himself is able to boast about his skill in mowing and ploughing (18.366–75): momentarily he comes across as much as a farm manager as a king.

By the seventh century BC the typical Greek *polis* had become an aristocracy, ruled by the members of a small elite linked by kinship. This was the end of the so-called Greek dark age: commercial activity was on the rise and greater wealth raised the aspirations of people on the fringes of power. Civil unrest (*stasis*) ensued in many Greek cities of the seventh and sixth centuries. This gave rise to a new political development: tyranny.

The modern notion of tyranny implies a certain harshness of rule. A Greek tyrant could be a harsh ruler, but was not necessarily so. We can define Greek tyranny in two different ways. Strictly speaking, a Greek tyrant had assumed power in the place of the traditional ruling class of the city. Such tyrants tended to claim popular support, but a questionable claim on power often made their position insecure. Hence, tyrants were typically accompanied by bodyguards to protect them from political rivals. This leads to the second definition of a tyrant, as a harsh, despotic king. While the second definition is more familiar to the modern world, one could be a Greek tyrant *qua* usurper without gaining a reputation for despotism. It was nevertheless possible to draw a distinction between kingship and tyranny as 'good' and 'bad' forms of monarchy (Aristotle would later do this, in the fourth century: see *Politics* 1279a-b). This distinction will be useful at some points in this book, although tragic poets did not employ these terms with Aristotelian precision. In particular, the word *tyrannos* (tyrant) can appear in an ideologically neutral sense in Greek tragedy, while in other forms of literature it had a more pejorative meaning.

By the fifth century, tyranny had been replaced in the cities of the Greek mainland by more egalitarian forms of government. Usually this meant some form of oligarchy, in which the rule of law was observed but only a wealthy class of citizens participated fully in government. Athens was different.

Athenian democracy

The Athenians expelled their last tyrants in 510, but this act gave rise to still more *stasis*. A solution came in the year 508/7 when the politician Cleisthenes gained the upper hand over his rivals. By reorganizing the citizen body (*dêmos*) at a local level and giving all members of this body the chance to participate in government, he was able to maintain his own power base and put an end to *stasis*. It was probably Cleisthenes who invented a further mechanism for reducing political dispute. Every year the Athenians met to decide whether to have an ostracism. If they decided yes, then a later vote (with the names scratched on *ostraka*, potsherds) was held to decide who should go. As long as at least 6,000 votes were cast, the man with the most votes had to leave Athens for ten years. His opponents were left to exercise more political influence than before. Finally, Cleisthenes replaced the old council of 400 with a new council (*boulê*). The *boulê* had 500 members and any citizen could put his name forward to serve on it.

The new Athens was soon to be tested in the battlefield, with great success. In 490 an Athenian army saw off the mighty Persians at Marathon. In 480 the Persians returned, by land and sea. In the intervening period the leading politician Themistocles had persuaded the Athenians to build a vast navy. A combined Greek force, nominally under Spartan command but really guided by Themistocles and containing large numbers of Athenian ships, beat the Persians against the odds at the Battle of Salamis.

The Athenians built on this success. Many of the Aegean islands, plus the coastal cities of Ionia (the west coast of modern Turkey) and the Bosporus joined an alliance with Athens against possible further Persian attack. Many of these cities became democracies themselves. As the money raised by this alliance was kept on the island of Delos, this alliance is known to modern scholarship as the Delian League. From 454 the money, known as the tribute, was taken to Athens itself. This money was to be spent on ships, on regular payments to Athenian citizens for public service and on a fine new collection of buildings on Athens' acropolis. The pretence of an equal alliance was over: Athens was an imperial power.

Meanwhile, the democracy had become more radical still. In 462/1 the Athenians, on the advice of Ephialtes, voted to end the power of the old aristocratic council that met on the Areopagus (the hill of Ares). This body was left with the role of a homicide court, while its old powers were divided between the assembly (*ekklêsia*), the *boulê* and the popular courts. These courts were presided over not by judges but by panels of jurors numbering hundreds at a time. Ephialtes' political ally Pericles proposed further measures to radicalise the democracy: pay for jury service and for serving on the *boulê*. This had two implications: the pay was not much (two obols, or a third of a skilled worker's daily wage, increased to three for jury service in 425) but it must have a made a difference to the really poor; and it provided an incentive for wide political participation.

A modern democracy gives its enfranchised citizens a regular opportunity to choose its leaders by ballot. Radical Athenian democracy, for all its association with slavery and its failure to recognize the rights of women, was far more democratic than that: this was a *direct* democracy, in which any citizen could speak or vote at regular assembly meetings. If a monarchy was ruled by one man and an oligarchy by a few, a democracy was a city where the *dêmos* was sovereign. The assembly did not literally represent the whole people: the Pnyx (the hilltop auditorium where the assembly met) could seat up to 6,000, a large number but still a minority of the citizens; and there were various ways in which the power of the assembly to do what it liked was limited.[6] Nevertheless, this assembly had the power to pass decrees and (in the fifth century) laws; to appoint generals and declare war. This did not reduce the need for political leaders: if anything their role became more important since this mass assembly needed informed proposals on which to vote. Real political power lay not in the holding of executive office but in the ability to speak to the assembly and persuade it to one's point of view.

This is not to say that there was no such thing as political office in Athens. Any one of a range of jobs, from public offices of various kinds to membership of the *boulê*, could be held by a citizen for one year at a time. Thus a central democratic idea was one of ruling in succession (compare Euripides, *Suppliants* 406–7, quoted and discussed on pages 121–4 below). Appointment to most of these offices was by lot, not vote – this was seen as the most democratic method: the rationale of a democracy is that anyone is able to rule; here was a method of choosing that allowed anyone who put his name forward to be appointed. The most notable exception to this rule was the annual election by vote of ten generals (perhaps the Athenians recognised the need for some skill in military strategy). In the fifth century, to be a general could be a matter of considerable political prestige.

The rise of Athens inevitably brought the Athenians into conflict with the established great power of Greece, their old ally Sparta. The so-called First Peloponnesian War (starting in about 460 and finally settled in 446) brought Corinth and eventually Sparta into conflict with the newly radicalised Athenians. The Spartans and their allies fought Athens again from 431 to 421 and from 415 until Athens' final defeat in 404. These two later conflicts were recorded by the historian Thucydides and are known collectively as the Second Peloponnesian War, or usually just the Peloponnesian War. The population of the city plummeted during this period due to the combined effects of battle and plague; and the Athenians only briefly, in the 370s, would come close to restoring their old empire. However, the city and a reformed democracy survived intact well into the fourth century. The democratic era was interrupted on just two occasions. In 411 a depleted Athenian assembly voted to hand over power to a body of 400, later expanded to 5,000; full democracy was restored within twelve months of the revolution. In 404 the victorious Spartans enforced a regime known as the Thirty Tyrants. Their rule was terrifying but brief.

Greek tragedy

Classical Athens was an extraordinary city in all sorts of ways. Rarely in European history has there been such a concentration of influential poets, historians, philosophers and other intellectuals in such a small space. The level of cultural activity must have been striking, but two things would have struck the visitor before anything else: one was the impressive collection of temples on the acropolis, the largest of which was the Parthenon; the other (if this visitor had come at the right time of year and looked just below the acropolis on the south side) was the largest annual gathering of Greeks: the audience at the dramatic festival known as the City Dionysia.

Given the methodology stated above, I should consider the composition of this audience before going any further – although there is no real agreement on many of the main issues. Let me first state what we appear to know for certain.

1. The audience was very large, numbering several thousands. Although few would take Plato's figure of 30,000 literally (Plato, *Symposium* 175e), modern estimates can be as high as 17,000 and no lower than 6,000. I shall take 14,000 as a realistic figure for the purposes of this book.[7]

2. There was a significant minority of foreigners in the audience (see pages 41–2 below). These included visitors from overseas and some of the great many metics living in the city.

3. But the majority of the spectators must have been Athenian citizens. This can be assumed since citizens formed the majority of the free population of the city and since comic poets feel able to address the audience as if they are the citizens of Athens (for example, at Aristophanes, *Clouds* 587). Sometimes the audience is addressed as men and boys (Aristophanes, *Peace* 50–3, compare *Clouds* 537–9), leading us to conclude that some citizens brought their sons to the theatre. Comedies at the Dionysia were performed on the same days and therefore to the same audiences as tragedy; thus comic evidence can be used to deduce who was in the tragic audience. (Note that in comedy the actors could address the audience directly; they never did in tragedy.)

4. Certain public officials and other dignitaries sat in special seats called *prohedriai*.[8]

Other points are more controversial.

5. Were citizens of all social classes represented equally in the audience? A theatre ticket cost two obols, the same amount a citizen earned for one day's jury service (at the pre-425 rate of pay). The ticket price may have put off some of the poorest citizens, most obviously small farmers who worked their own land. Some of these men lived as much as a day's walk from the city and probably outside the cash economy. By the fourth century at the latest citizens received a public dole, intended to be spent on theatre attendance, from what is known as the Theoric Fund; however, it is unclear that this fund existed in the fifth century, the period covered by this

book. Even so, we cannot exclude large numbers of ordinary citizens from our idea of the audience: a high proportion of the citizen population could be considered poor (maybe half were unable to maintain their own armour and weapons and so fight in the army: see pages 92–3 below); therefore the poor must have attended the theatre in numbers, even if the rich were disproportionately represented.[9]

6. It is possible that slaves could have attended, but highly unlikely that many did.[10]

7. Were there women in the audience? This remains a topic on which there is no scholarly consensus. It is noticeable that women spectators are hardly ever acknowledged in comedy (Aristophanes, *Peace* 962–7 and *Lysistrata* 1050–1 are possible exceptions). A plausible explanation that has been given is that, although women were there, they were usually excluded from addresses to the audience by comic actors and choruses; there is a difference between the actual and a notional audience.[11] There does not appear to have been any bar on female attendance (as indeed at any Athenian religious festival);[12] this, however, should not lead us to conclude that many women actually came. Those women who did attend were more likely to be resident foreigners than Athenian women, the wives and mothers of citizens: this is because Athenian women tended to keep themselves apart in public.[13] Any Athenian women that did attend may well have sat separately from the men, perhaps at the back.[14]

One can broadly, if tentatively, conclude that the audience was a large and mixed body of people from almost all walks of Greek life, of which Athenian citizens together with their sons – future citizens – made up the largest component, and foreigners a notice-able minority. This was a more diverse gathering than was seen in the democratic assembly, which was attended by adult male citizens only. We can see how Plato in the fourth century could describe drama as 'a kind of rhetoric addressed to such a *dêmos* as is composed of children together with women and men both slave and free' (Plato, *Gorgias* 502d-e, compare *Laws* 817c).

The Dionysia was a religious festival in honour of the god Dionysus. Various rural Dionysia were held in midwinter across Attica (the territory of Athens). The Dionysia held in spring is generally distin-guished by the term Great, or City Dionysia. From some time in the late sixth century this became a dramatic festival at which trag-edies and (later) comedies were staged. From the mid-fifth century dramas were also presented at a festival called the Lenaia (in our month of January or February, also in honour of Dionysus) and increasingly at some of the rural Dionysia.

The Lenaia was a large festival, in which mass audiences were entertained over several days; the City Dionysia was in several respects even larger. First, the City Dionysia was almost certainly longer, lasting for five days (although this was probably reduced to four during the Peloponnesian War). A longer festival admitted more people – assuming that not everyone went every day. If the audience on any day numbered 14,000, we might guess that between 20,000 and 30,000 citizens and others attended parts of the Dionysia each year. Someone who attended the whole festival could see a tetralogy by each of three tragic poets (four plays consisting of three tragedies and a more humorous satyr play, so called because it had a chorus of satyrs); he would see five comedies, and competitions for men and boys in dithyrambic (choral) dancing.

Second, the City Dionysia was more expensive. Actors and poets were paid at public expense, while some of the richest men in the city paid for the choruses. These men were known as *chorêgoi*.

Tetralogies were produced in competition with each other and victory was a matter of great prestige for both poet and *chorêgos*. *Chorêgoi* sponsored productions at other festivals, as well as comic and dithyrambic choruses at the Dionysia, but the *chorêgia* for a tetralogy at the Dionysia carried the greatest prestige and so was probably awarded to one of the wealthiest men.[15] The sums could be immense. A defendant in an Athenian trial whose speech has come down to us (number 21 among the speeches of Lysias) wishes to demonstrate his good public works to a citizen jury. He begins by listing the amounts he has spent as *chorêgos* at various festivals: 800 drachmae here, 2,000 drachmae there; but the largest sum, 30 minae (3,000 drachmae, or 18,000 obols!), was spent on a tragic chorus.

Thirdly and lastly, the City Dionysia was probably broader in appeal. Held at a time of year when the seas had just become suitable for regular sailing, it was an international festival, an opportunity for Athens to promote itself among the other Greek *poleis*: see the next chapter.

Tragedy probably began in the sixth century and had its origins in choral performances. The revolutionary move attributed to the poet-actor Thespis was to stand apart from the chorus members and play the part of an individual hero. This opened up dramatic possibilities. Consider a possible scene based on the beginning of book 18 of Homer's *Iliad*. Instead of just presenting a choral performance on the death of Patroclus, a poet could write a dialogue in which Achilles mourns the death of his comrade in conversation with the sea nymphs and plans his revenge. According to Aristotle (*Poetics* 1449a15–18), Aeschylus added a second actor and Sophocles a third. These were two of the three most celebrated tragic poets; the third was Sophocles' contemporary, Euripides. Their combined long careers spanned the period of Athenian imperial power, almost up to its eventual demise. Aeschylus died in 456/5 when he was nearly seventy. Sophocles died in 406 at the age of ninety and Euripides, who was around ten years younger, died less than a year before that.

Most or all of the thirty tragedies to have survived complete from the fifth century are by these three. We have one complete trilogy, the *Oresteia*, by Aeschylus and three other single plays. A fourth, *Prometheus Bound*, is traditionally attributed to Aeschylus but may be by a later poet. Seven tragedies and much of one satyr play by Sophocles survive, a tiny sample of the 120 or so dramas that he wrote and produced. From Euripides we have a more representative selection: sixteen tragedies, one satyr play (*Cyclops*) and one play (*Alcestis*) that defies categorisation by genre. A seventeenth tragedy, *Rhesus*, is attributed to Euripides but was probably written in the fourth century. It is easy to write about Greek tragedy as if these were the only poets, and I hope to be forgiven if I do so in this book. We know of several others and have fragments from their plays. It is also too easy to think of these thirty-odd plays as the complete works of the canonical tragedians. Far more has been lost than has survived, and we have no complete works from the early careers of any of these poets.

Tragedy as a genre can be defined by form and content. As for content, by no means all Greek tragedies have sad endings, but most are concerned at some point with intense suffering. In addition, tragic poets are rarely shy of including the sort of unsettling events that Homer certainly avoids, most notoriously intra-familial killing. The plots of tragedies usually drew on myth, although some of the earlier poets produced 'historical' tragedies, as we shall see in the next chapter. As for form, tragedies (like comedies) were written in verse. The choruses and other lyric passages were set to music. The audience therefore had plenty to hear. They also had plenty to see: the actors wore masks and outsize, colourful costumes; violent scenes were described by messengers, not dramatised, but the bodies of the dead generally appeared on stage soon afterwards.

On two grounds it appears that only Athens of the Greek city-states could have developed and promoted drama to this extent. First, the democracy that began around or soon after the beginning of the dramatic festivals indirectly promoted free speech among its citizens. The Athenians were conscious of their tendency to exercise *parrhêsia*, which literally means 'saying everything'. Their behaviour in all aspects of city life was characterised by talk. So there seems to be something distinctively Athenian about a genre in which several competing voices are heard at once. Second, in few other cities could be found the concentration of public and private wealth that was needed to sustain an annual display on this scale.

The organisation of the City Dionysia suggests that this was in some way a political organ alongside the assembly, *boulê* and law courts: the city appointed the poets and *chorêgoi*, and the normal business of the city was suspended while a predominantly citizen audience attended the festival. The festival therefore was a public occasion both in its administration and (arguably) in the audience's sense of shared experience. (Again, I am not sure that this meant shared political views.) At the same time, the cosmopolitan nature of the audience and the holiday atmosphere made the theatre a less usual type of political organ: more conducive to political reflection than decision-making.

It is therefore inevitable that much of this book will be concerned with the relevance of tragic politics to the Athenians at various points in the fifth century. However, the tragic poets seem rarely to have been preoccupied narrowly with Athenian politics, in a way that fifth-century comic poets frequently were. Nor, for all the success of democracy, did the Greeks share the modern western assumption that this is the only way to govern. All of the fifth-century tragedies that survive were first performed at the City Dionysia, which was, we have seen, an international festival. Tragedy needed to be broader in its appeal. As will become clear in the next three chapters, the most basic sense in which tragedy is political lies in a concern with the life of Greek *polis* in general.

CHAPTER 2

SOME VIEWS, THEIR
IMPLICATIONS

A very modern controversy

Few topics in Greek literature have been as hotly debated in recent
years as the political function of Greek tragedy. The purpose of this
chapter is to demonstrate and criticise six of the more important
critical approaches of the last fifty years. Each approach is illustrated
with a discussion of one or two plays and the chapter concludes with
a critical summary of Aeschylus' *Oresteia*. Three broad points will
become clear: the number and variety of modern political readings
of Greek tragedy; the differing politics of several individual plays;
that all this is crucial to our understanding of Greek drama and
political culture. The growing heat of the debate only reflects the
importance of the topic.

One problem that will emerge concerns how we define 'the political' in tragedy. Anyone reading a tragedy politically will adopt some
definition or other, whether this is made explicit or not. In the next
chapter I attempt my own working definition; in this chapter I hope
to show what available definitions there are. One fairly strict sense
of 'the political' concerns events at governmental level; a broader
view might consider politics in terms of community and human
interaction. There is plenty of scope for movement between these
two extremes, although the trend in recent scholarship has been
towards the broader view.

The historicist approach

Perhaps the most obvious way of approaching politics in tragedy is what can be called the 'historicist' line. A well known and easily accessible example is Anthony J. Podlecki's book *The Political Background of Aeschylean Tragedy*, originally published in 1966. Podlecki aims to place the tragedies of Aeschylus in the immediate historical context of their first performance. He purports to relate some of the dramas to contemporary or recent events in the political life of the Athenians. This approach seems far easier to take with Aeschylus' earliest surviving tragedy, *Persians*, than with any of the others. This play was produced in 472 BC and is a tragedy, from a supposed Persian perspective, about a recent event: the Greek victory over the Persians at Salamis in 480. *Persians* is thus the only surviving example of a 'historical' tragedy, a genre that may not have occurred with great frequency and in any case died out with this play or soon after. All the other tragedies that we have, including five or six by Aeschylus, draw on myth. The assumption behind Podlecki's book is that in his mythical dramas Aeschylus was no less keen to refer, or at least allude, to contemporary events and issues.

At this stage we should note one thing never found in Greek tragedy, and that is full-scale political allegory.[16] There is no tragic *Animal Farm*. One aspect of the circumstances of tragedy's performance suggests why this might be the case; it can be illustrated by an early example. In the late 490s a poet named Phrynichus produced a tragedy, *The Capture of Miletus*, about the Persian devastation of that city in 494. Miletus was an Ionian city, with which Athens had close ties and which Athens might have been expected to defend. Phrynichus was fined heavily by the Athenians for reminding them of their own misfortunes (see Herodotus 6.21). This event on its own does not explain the demise of historical tragedy, a type of play that both Phrynichus and Aeschylus were still presenting twenty years later; but it does show how vulnerable a poet could be to the will of a people that took its drama – as well as itself – very seriously indeed. This in turn helps to explain why tragic poets preferred the safe distance of mythology as a context for their plays (on political aspects of this heroic setting, see ch. 3).

This presents a stark contrast with fifth-century comedy, in which individual Athenians (though, again, rarely the Athenians as a whole) were satirised regularly, frequently and sometimes at great length.[17] In fact, it is in a comedy that we *do* find ancient Greek political allegory: *Knights* by Aristophanes. The difference from any tragedy is instructive. This play is a highly sophisticated allegory in which the city of Athens is represented as a farm, the people of Athens as its master, and various politicians as a devious collection of slaves. Two of these slaves appear to represent Nicias and Demosthenes, members of the board of ten elected generals. A third slave, named the Paphlagonian, clearly corresponds to Cleon, the leading politician in the year 424 when *Knights* was first produced.[18] Even before we hear his name we can tell that this is Cleon from the repeated references to leather-tanning (his father's trade), to the campaign at Pylos (his recent military triumph) and to his aggressive manner. Thus the nature of the allegory was made abundantly clear to an audience that was already expecting to hear jokes directed against public figures. Contrast this with heroic tragedy, where the audience expected to be taken away from the present unless clearly directed otherwise, and we can take the following as a general principle: any contemporary reference in tragedy must be made obvious so as not to escape the original audience, let alone the modern reader. It remains possible that a poet with an axe to grind could disguise his message so that only those in the know could hear it; but if there were hidden allegory in any surviving Greek drama, we are so much the less likely to discover it with the limited historical evidence available to us.

Podlecki is well aware of the dangers of a historicist approach. He is cautious in discussing the tragedies in two respects: (1) he does not accept every possible historicist reading offered by his predecessors and, in addition, is careful to avoid reading political allegory into tragedy; (2) he is sensitive to broader issues and political ideas not necessarily of exclusive interest to the audience in the year of first production. Thus, in his discussion of *Prometheus Bound* (which he takes to be genuinely by Aeschylus), with respect to (1), he does not accept that the tyrannical character of Zeus is supposed to represent any contemporary tyrant; but regarding (2), he does see the play as among other things a discussion of the nature of tyranny. Thus *Prometheus Bound* becomes one of the very earliest pieces of political theory in European literature.

Podlecki's ideas are exemplified in his discussion of Aeschylus' *Suppliants*. In this play, the daughters of Danaus who make up the chorus are seeking asylum in Argos. They are on the run from their cousins, the fifty sons of Aegyptus, who wish to marry them against their will. The Argives under their king Pelasgus agree to protect the women, even though it means certain war. One does not need to look far for the political relevance of this play to an Athenian audience: despite its heroic setting and apparent monarchy, this Argos is a democracy. Pelasgus' power appears to go no further than that of a fifth-century Athenian politician: the ability to persuade the people in assembly to vote in support of his proposals (see further pages 86–7 below). The nature of Pelasgus' political influence and the means by which he uses it – successfully persuading the people to vote for an action that will lead them to endanger their own lives in battle – make the political environment of this drama clear. We are also provided with some insight into the predicament and the behaviour of the democratic politician.

Podlecki provides a useful discussion of these last few points, but his historicist approach takes him further. The scope of this kind of reading is greatly enhanced if one knows the year in which a play was first performed. When Podlecki was writing his book in the 1960s the recent discovery of a papyrus fragment had allowed scholars to place the play in the 460s BC, and not in the 490s as was previously thought. With reasonable certainly, one can go further and date the play to the spring of 463.[19] Podlecki accepts this date and draws our attention to the precise political circumstances of the Greek world of the time. The following year, 462, saw a significant Athenian alliance with Argos. By making this alliance the Athenians effectively thumbed their noses both at Sparta, a long-standing enemy of Argos, and at Cimon, a previously influential Athenian politician who had been attempting to forge closer links with the Spartans. Cimon's political fate was sealed soon after when he was ostracised (see ch. 1 on ostracism). We shall see before the end of this chapter that there are clear references to the Argive alliance in Aeschylus' *Eumenides*, produced in 458. Podlecki sees *Suppliants* as an indication that the Athenians, with Aeschylus' approval, were already considering such an alliance in 463. There is less in the text to support this than is found in *Eumenides*. For Podlecki, the crucial point is that the democracy in which the drama is set is more than a reflection of the Athenian system; it is a clear celebration of the real Argos, by then a democracy also. Podlecki goes further still: the Argives' protection of the Danaid women puts us in mind of Argos' most famous recent foreign visitor. Themistocles, the hero of Salamis, was the leading politician in Athens until his ostracism in around 471. He began his exile in Argos and used that city as a base from which to contrive against the Spartans. By the time of the first performance of *Suppliants* he had moved on again, as we shall see shortly.

There are many advantages to Podlecki's approach. It is rooted in close reference to the text of Aeschylus and the historical evidence. He does not push the historical agenda to breaking point. The connections he makes put us in mind of political issues as well as political events: *Prometheus Bound* makes us think of tyranny, *Suppliants* of democracy. Most of all, the political context that he considers is an immediate one. He is not satisfied with making vague connections between the democracy of *Suppliants* and an Athenian democracy that lasted for nearly two hundred years from the late sixth century, as if politics never changed over that period. *Suppliants* ought to reflect the live political issues of the 460s more than, say, the 360s.

The disadvantages of Podlecki's approach fall broadly into two areas, both of which have been illuminated by trends in criticism since the time when his book first appeared. First of all, it has become a cliché of modern literary scholarship – and not just in Greek literature – that a work of fiction cannot be used as evidence for the views of the author. This view can be taken rather too far, but it has been a useful corrective to some studies, which try to create a biography of the author based on fictive texts; firmer conclusions can usually be gained from a consideration of the text on its own merits. When we come to drama, a genre that allows many voices to be heard, none of which necessarily belong to the author, then the risks of the 'biographical' approach are only too plain. If we cannot tell from the text of a play in which Pelasgus appears whether we should approve wholly of the king's actions, we are even less likely to find out the author's view on Themistocles, who does not appear. A few tragedies still allow us to infer an author's opinion on particular issues, for example Aeschylus' *Eumenides* (see the end of this chapter for Podlecki's view on this play). But someone writing Podlecki's book for the first time now would be more likely to identify issues in the plays of interest, generally, to Aeschylus' *audience* (this is essentially what I try to do in this book). The conclusions might not in fact be very different but they would lose their close association with the personality of the poet. Whether an audience-based approach seems even less rooted in the text depends on your point of view: the poet, after all, has left us a text; the audience has not. On the other hand, it is worth remembering that these plays were produced in competition before a vast audience, most of whom were citizens and whom the poet would be anxious to please – one way of doing this was to present views that chimed with the audience's own.

The second disadvantage does not invalidate Podlecki's approach, but it does reveal the scope of his inquiry. Podlecki takes a particular view of what counts as historical and, consequently, an equally particular idea of the political. For Podlecki, history is political history and politics are high politics: his concern is with political *events*. This allows him to take in some important political issues, as we have seen. But there is far more that can be said about tragic politics. A modern social historian would remark on Podlecki's failure to consider the position of women and slaves, who feature in most tragedies, sometimes more prominently than free men (I consider a reading of tragedy that satisfies this criticism below). Further, Podlecki does not always look at the whole picture when it comes to issues of interest to Athenian citizens. We saw in ch. 1 that the ancient Greek equivalent to our 'politics' is *ta politika* – the affairs of the *polis*. These did not stop with the deeds of great men, even though tragedy, with its heroic setting, is well placed to focus on this aspect of politics. Nor did they stop with the merits of democracy over tyranny, the conduct of an assembly meeting or whether to ally oneself with another city – important though each of these issues were. Politics had to do with how to run a city, but also with how to be a citizen, a *politês*. The vast majority of Athenians in the audience would never be political or military leaders, but they were obliged to play their part in the democracy: to vote in the assembly, serve on juries, fill various magistracies; also to fight in the line of battle or row with the fleet.

A popular idea of tragedy was of the poet as teacher. We saw in ch. 1 that this idea underpins the quarrel between Aeschylus and Euripides in Aristophanes' *Frogs*. One thing the Aristophanic Aeschylus says is that his play *Seven Against Thebes* (which has survived from antiquity) instilled a warlike spirit into the citizens (*Frogs* 1021–2). There are grounds for not taking this remark too seriously as an appraisal of the political worth of the play. First of all, Aeschylus goes on to suggest the 'hero Lamachus' (1039) as an example of a warlike Athenian inspired by watching his tragedies. Lamachus, an Athenian general killed in battle in 414 BC, is ridiculed at length by Aristophanes in his *Acharnians* (produced 425) as a general who adopts extremes of belligerence and promotes war against the interests of the Athenians. The same phrase, 'hero Lamachus', is in fact used ironically at line 575 of *Acharnians*. (On the other hand, Lamachus does not seem to have been ridiculed in the same way after his death: he is mentioned in respectful terms at line 841 of Aristophanes' *Women at the Thesmophoria*, produced 411; *Frogs* was produced six years later still, in 405). Secondly (as Podlecki points out), a lesson in how to be warlike would have seemed more important to the Athenians in 405, at the climax of the Peloponnesian War, than in 467, the date of *Seven Against Thebes*. The above is not designed to provide a proper discussion of the politics of *Seven Against Thebes*, but it does allow us to make a point about the scope of Podlecki's study of tragedy. Aristophanes, whose idea of political tragedy had to do with the education of good citizens, suggests *Seven Against Thebes* as a model drama, however humorously. Podlecki discusses the politics of *Seven Against Thebes* but, because he defines political drama principally as drama that makes reference to political events, concludes that it is 'the least political of the surviving plays'.[20]

A further result of Podlecki's approach is that, although he eschews political allegory and does not try to look for historical *individuals* behind tragic characters, he can perhaps look too hard for historical *events*. Take the *Suppliants* and Themistocles. Podlecki does not try to equate fifty Egyptian virgins with one exiled Athenian general, but he does suggest that their circumstances are similar. He admits some of the shortcomings of this view, which I attempt to list in full here. The suppliants of Aeschylus' play are on the run from the sons of Aegyptus; Themistocles at the time of his stay in Argos was on the run from nobody (ostracism was a political short straw drawn by individuals in certain years, and was not a punishment for anything). The Argives seem set on harbouring the suppliants no matter what; Themistocles left Argos at the first sign of trouble from Athens (see Thucydides 1.136 – by this point he *was* on the run and was soon to become a suppliant himself). The acceptance of suppliants in the play requires a vote in the assembly in the face of certain war; Themistocles was never a suppliant in Argos, did not need the city's formal permission to stay and, at the time of his arrival, put no Argive lives at risk by his presence.

To summarise. The identification of historical allusions in tragedy can be risky: one can look too hard. If on the other hand one exercises some judgement, such observations can lead to broader insights into ancient political drama. The implied definition of 'political' that underlies this approach imposes limits on the inquiry. Such limits have their methodological use, giving definition to the conclusions, but there is far more that can be said.

A broader definition of the political

Most of the concerns with Podlecki's approach that I raise here are raised by C.W. Macleod in his article, 'Politics and the *Oresteia*' (published posthumously in 1982). Aeschylus' *Oresteia* is a trilogy, comprising the tragedies *Agamemnon*, *Libation Bearers* and *Eumenides*. I will discuss political readings of the *Oresteia* more fully at the end of this chapter. However, it will help to summarise the trilogy before going any further. What follows is necessarily brief and misses out some important scenes and characters, but it serves our present purpose. Many readers will be familiar with the plays already and may prefer to skip the next paragraph.

The first play opens just after the fall of Troy, as the elders of Argos (the chorus of the play) and Queen Clytemnestra await the return of the commander of the Greek forces, her husband Agamemnon. The elders assert their belief in the divine order of the universe and especially in a principle of justice articulated later in the play (line 1564) as 'the one who acts must suffer'. This principle appears to place an obligation on the immediate family of the victim to ensure that suffering ensues. From this view it follows that an act of vengeance can be an act of justice. However, the men of the chorus remember that just before he went to Troy Agamemnon sacrificed his own daughter Iphigenia to the goddess Artemis in order to provide a fair wind for his fleet. The question appears to be: if the doer suffers, what will Agamemnon suffer when he returns to his wife? And where will it all end? Clytemnestra kills her husband, invoking justice for Iphigenia. In *Libation Bearers* Orestes, the son of Agamemnon and Clytemnestra, returns from exile. He has been presented with a dilemma: he cannot avenge his father without killing his mother. On the earlier advice of the Delphic oracle, he kills Clytemnestra. He is pursued by the Furies, ancient guardians of the vengeance model of justice. The third play is called *Eumenides*, the name now given to the Furies, who are now played by the chorus. They pursue Orestes to Athens, where Orestes stands trial before the council of the Areopagus. (In real life, the powers of this council had been severely limited in 462/1 BC, just a few years before the first performance of the *Oresteia*: it is a point of debate whether Aeschylus' celebration of the Areopagus celebrates or condemns this move.) With Athene as its president, the court acquits Orestes. A potentially endless cycle of vengeance has been stopped. In addition, a judicial model of justice has (not replaced but) regulated the old system of personal vengeance.

Macleod's article falls essentially into two parts. The first part criticises the historicist reading, not of Podlecki, but of E.R. Dodds. Macleod takes the passages from Aeschylus' *Eumenides* that are most often cited as referring to historical events and examines them one by one. He concludes that Aeschylus alludes to only two historical events: the Argive alliance and the reduction of the powers of the Areopagus (on both, see the end of this chapter). Even on these two issues, he argues (against the position of Podlecki) that Aeschylus is not adopting a partisan line. Aeschylus' message, says Macleod, is intended to be more universal and less rooted in his own times. If the first part of Macleod's article is destructive, the second is constructive. He builds his own political reading of *Eumenides* around the Greek words *dikê* (justice) and *timê* (honour, respect), which appear in various forms throughout the text of the trilogy. The idea of *dikê* is central to the *Oresteia* and has been discussed frequently both before and after Macleod. I mention an aspect of it very briefly in the next paragraph. *Timê* in the *Oresteia*, says Macleod, means respect for social institutions. Thus the killing of Agamemnon shows a lack of respect for the institutions of marriage, the household, kingship and generalship. At the end of the trilogy, the institution of a judicial model of justice is based on respect for – even fear of – the law and its new guardians, the Eumenides. (See *Eumenides* 696–703, quoted on page 62 below; on the virtue of fear in the city, see further pages 95–6.) The second half of Macleod's article, therefore, broadly demonstrates his definition of the political in tragedy: 'a concern with human beings as a part of a community'.

Macleod is also anxious to preserve Aeschylus' reputation as a dramatist. Podlecki is certainly at pains in his introduction to say that the presence of historical references does not diminish the plays as literature. What is different in Macleod's method is that he incorporates dramatic concerns fully into his inquiry. If one views the trilogy as a whole, says Macleod, we can see that the issues associated in the *Eumenides* with the Argive alliance and the Areopagus are parts of wider concerns that span the whole work; these concerns are as important dramatically as politically. For instance, when in the first play Clytemnestra uses the language of *dikê* (justice) to defend the killing of Agamemnon, its use is highly problematic. When the word appears again in *Eumenides*, in association with the council of the Areopagus, Aeschylus is not making a narrow political point; rather, it is shown (dramatically) that irregularities in *dikê* have been corrected and (politically) that this is how good cities behave. To dramatise a trial before the Areopagus council, says Macleod, is not to make a partisan point so soon after its powers had been cut but to portray Athenian justice as ideal and Athens as the ideal city.

Macleod's approach to politics in tragedy has many advantages. Principally, his idea of the political, as 'a concern with human beings as part of a community', is far broader than Podlecki's and therefore opens up greater room for discussion. This definition is perhaps of greater importance to the thousands of ordinary Athenians and other Greeks in tragedy's original audience; and it makes greater sense in a discussion of tragedy, which tended to adopt a more lofty, universal perspective than comedy. Secondly, like Podlecki, Macleod bases his observations on close reference to the text and therefore forms a useful interpretation of the play on whatever level: political, historical or literary. Thirdly, he never allows us to forget that this is a work of literature. Dramatic concerns are never far from his interpretation of the political.

There are only two real drawbacks to Macleod's views as stated in his article. First, just as Podlecki looks a little too hard for historical events, Macleod puts a little too much effort into diverting attention away from them. For this reason, the first part of his paper is not the unqualified success that the second part surely is. Macleod's starting assumption, that tragic poets tend not to make topical references, is correct. *Eumenides*, however, is a tragedy unusually rooted in the exact time of its first production.[21] Most especially, this was a time of animosity between the political tendencies represented by Cimon and Ephialtes. While Macleod acknowledges that reference is made to the Argive alliance and the Areopagus council, he denies that Aeschylus has a position on these issues. But these were two matters on which it was difficult to be neutral in 458 BC: this may be one place where we *can* deduce the poet's own view. On this particular point, Podlecki's view seems more enlightening: see the last section of this chapter.

The second possible criticism of Macleod is harder to make because it involves negotiating a grey area between the social and the purely political. The strength of Macleod's definition is its breadth, but we must guard against too much breadth in case the definition ceases to define. The idea of 'human beings as part of a community' allows us to differentiate social drama from other drama, but there is surely something a little more special about the *political*. While there are a great many dramas in which interaction takes place among more than a handful of people, not all of these can be called political plays. What then makes some drama especially political? It is possible to present a play in which a woman kills her husband as a purely social drama (Sophocles' *Women of Trachis* is an example). One can even write a play in which this woman is thus seen to offend against the institutions of marriage and the household, and still not make a political statement. It is true that in *Agamemnon* the husband is not just the head of a household but also the king of a city and the commander of an army, as both Aeschylus and Macleod remind us; but Aeschylus did not have to write his trilogy this way. Sophocles and Euripides both dramatise the killing of Clytemnestra but in different ways amplify the role of Electra (who gives the title to each play); in this way they make these dramas rather more domestic in scope (on this point, see page 67 below).

While Macleod could do more to tease out the purely political from the merely social, he comes close to making such a distinction in two ways. First, the *Oresteia* is concerned throughout with issues of justice and therefore law. The language used from the beginning of *Agamemnon* is frequently the language of the Athenian law court, as Macleod points out. Now, the existence of a Greek law rested on the *polis* that created it. (For the moment I am disregarding the paradoxical notion of 'unwritten laws', on which see the discussion of Sophocles' *Antigone* in ch. 4.) Thus, while the killing of a husband can be the subject of a purely domestic drama, any mention of the legality of that deed brings it into the political sphere. In fact, the *Oresteia* could be said to dramatise that journey into the political sphere, as we shall see in ch. 3. The justice-as-vengeance model could survive in the heroic world before the rise of the classical *polis*, as for example in Homeric epic; the judicial model requires the authority of the city. Second, Macleod's concern is frequently with institutions. Some of these institutions – marriage, the household – are not on their own political, but most of them are: kingship, law, and so on.

Perhaps the most telling difference between Macleod and many other writers on this subject is that he makes a conscious effort to define 'the political'. The definition that he adopts ('a concern with human beings as part of a community') allows him to draw some important conclusions not just on concepts of *dikê* and *timê* but also on their political meaning to the Greeks. This also allows Macleod to unlock greater meaning in the Oresteian trilogy. But, while Podlecki's point of view narrows the scope for political readings of tragedy, Macleod's definition makes it too broad. We shall return to this problem of breadth later in this chapter, and I attempt to solve it in ch. 3.

The democratic assumption

Perhaps the most influential political reading of tragedy of recent years is that of Simon Goldhill. His approach takes the festive context of the original performance of tragedy fully into account. It will be remembered from ch. 1 that nearly all of the extant fifth-century tragedies were performed at the larger of two annual festivals: the Great, or City Dionysia. We already know that the City Dionysia was a massive event, lasting four or five days; we know that the city paid the poets and the leading actors; and we know that, although the choruses were paid for by rich private individuals (*chorêgoi*), these individuals were appointed by a magistrate on behalf of the city (see the Aristotelian *Constitution of the Athenians*, ch. 56). The City Dionysia was a civic occasion before it even started. Goldhill's special focus is on the ceremonies that may have taken place at the start of particular days of the festival. I list them now in the order in which Goldhill discusses them.

1. The ten elected generals of the city came forward to pour libations to the gods.[22]

2. Every year, the members of the Delian League contributed a tribute – a sum of money – to the Athenian public purse. From 454 the tribute was brought to Athens at the time of the Dionysia. According to one source used by Goldhill, this tribute was divided into talents (a high denomination of currency) and brought into the theatre in front of the audience.[23]

3. Proclamations were made of the award of honorific crowns to individuals who had benefited the city.[24]

4. The orphans of Athenian soldiers killed in battle were brought up and educated at public expense. When they reached

eighteen years of age, they paraded in full battle dress in front of the audience at that year's Dionysia.[25]

The significance of these ceremonies to Goldhill's work can be summarised in three respects. First, the City Dionysia was 'fundamentally and essentially a festival of the democratic *polis*' and 'to be in the audience is above all *to play the role of democratic citizen*'.[26] In ceremony number 1 the men pouring the libations were 'the ten most powerful military and political leaders' in the city.[27] Second, the ceremonies were a public advertisement for the power and prestige of Athens. Ceremony number 2 underlines not only the great wealth of Athens but also the size of its empire and the strength of its military, which allowed it to collect such wealth from nominally allied states. Third, an example was being set to the citizens. Crowns were presented, according to Demosthenes, in order to encourage other citizens to serve the city well (*On the Crown* 120 – but Demosthenes *would* say that: his aim is to justify a disputed decree awarding a crown to him). That the young men in ceremony number 4 had been brought up at public expense shows how much the Athenians thought of men who died for their city; that they paraded in full military dress suggests that they could be expected to make the same sacrifice.

Goldhill then integrates the plays into his argument: the plays are political in that they make the citizen think about how to live in a *polis*. The festival, argues Goldhill, asserted the prestige of the particular *polis* that hosted it and celebrated the worth of its citizens. As for the plays themselves, it can be objected that by no means all tragedies celebrate the *polis* all the time, nor do they always present citizens that do their best for the city. This, argues Goldhill, is because the political function of the plays is to ask questions of democratic values, ceremonial expressions of which the audience members have just seen.

An example Goldhill gives is *Philoctetes*, written and produced by Sophocles in 409. In this play, the hero Philoctetes has been marooned on a desert island for ten years while the Trojan War is in progress. This situation seems set to change following a prophecy that the Greeks will only take Troy when Philoctetes, who is equipped with the bow and arrows of Heracles, is restored to the army. A mission is sent to bring him back, led by Odysseus. However, it was on Odysseus' advice that Philoctetes was abandoned before (his leg had been bitten by a snake and his constant cries of agony were irritating the Greeks and had created a distraction from sacrifice). Philoctetes hates Odysseus and will not do anything that pleases him and the army. Odysseus therefore sends in Neoptolemus, the son of the dead Achilles. Since Neoptolemus was not part of the original fleet that sailed, Philoctetes has no quarrel with him. Neoptolemus is ordered to deceive Philoctetes, pretending also to have fallen out with the Greek army at Troy; thus he will win Philoctetes' trust and take him away, supposedly back home but actually to Troy. Now, the Odysseus of this play is a figure of authority but clearly an unattractive character. The propensity to lie and deceive, which is such a distinctive feature in Homer's *Odyssey*, is here (as elsewhere in tragedy) turned into a quality that we must reject. Neoptolemus from the outset is uneasy with the plan to deceive Philoctetes – but he does what he is told. As he gets to know Philoctetes he pities him and becomes his friend in fact as well as name. He first tells Philoctetes the truth and finally agrees to take the hero home. Odysseus' authority and tactics have been rejected. Only the intervention of the deified hero Heracles persuades them both to head for Troy instead.

For an audience that has just witnessed the parade of the war orphans, suggests Goldhill, *Philoctetes* would have been especially interesting. These are the sons of men who put the interests of the collective – the army or city – before their own safety. *Philoctetes* is a play in which a man of about the same age as the war orphans chooses, for good reasons, to place the interests of an individual above those of the army. Thus the drama raises questions about the ideology of acting to benefit the city.

The main advantage of Goldhill's approach is that it sets the tragedies in the context of their first performance. This context – the festive one – reflects a different emphasis from Podlecki's historical context and was even more immediate to the audience sitting in the theatre at the time. Further, Goldhill gives due emphasis to the relationship between the city and the festival. The City Dionysia was not a private affair: it was arranged and partly paid for by the city. Given, additionally, that the dramas frequently raised political issues, we can conclude that the festival became a part of the city's political mechanism. For anyone writing on the subject in Goldhill's wake, it is (rightly) impossible to ignore the importance of the festivals in which the plays were produced. Goldhill is also broadly correct when he says that tragedy 'problematizes' the *polis*, although it seems he has Athens chiefly in mind: this, it will be seen, is too restrictive.

However, there are several problems with Goldhill's thesis. In his critique of Goldhill's work, Jasper Griffin points out the difficulty of arguing 'from the character of part of a festival ... to that of the festival as a whole'.[28] In other words, the importance of these ceremonies to Goldhill rests on the assumption that the audience would have kept them in the front of their minds as they proceeded to watch the plays; we simply cannot know whether they did this. Further, we cannot be certain that the ceremonies preceded every presentation of tragedy. The City Dionysia lasted for five days, which were probably reduced to four during the Peloponnesian War. In any sensible reconstruction of the programme, tragic performances began at dawn on the mornings of three of these four or five days.[29] Can we seriously assume that the four ceremonies started every one of these three days? More likely it was just the first one.

Further doubts surround the proclamation of crowns, for which all the evidence comes from the fourth century. It may be that such a proclamation honoured a deserving fifth-century Athenian, in front of the audience of the plays in question; but if so it seems surprising that we do not hear about it in the literary evidence. In fact, the orator Aeschines offers examples of fifth-century military heroes who were *not* crowned (Aeschines, *Against Ctesiphon* 178–81). Even in the time of Aeschines' speech (330 BC), the award of a crown by the *dêmos* to a citizen in the theatre emerges as a rare event, the subject of a protracted legal dispute. Aeschines' speech is a legal challenge to Ctesiphon's assembly proposal to proclaim a crown for Demosthenes in the theatre at the City Dionysia. Most of the speech concentrates on Demosthenes' record in public life but part of it focuses on the legality of the award itself (*Against Ctesiphon* 9–48, of which 32–48 is the important section here). One of the laws he cites (at *Against Ctesiphon* 32) appears to have said that crowns awarded to citizens by the *dêmos* could only be proclaimed in the assembly on the Pnyx; likewise, a crown awarded by the *boulê* had to be proclaimed in *bouleuterion*, the building where that body met. This law allowed only for the proclamation in the theatre – duly sanctioned by the *dêmos* – of crowns awarded by other cities. Therefore, argues Aeschines, the kind of award that Ctesiphon has proposed, by the *dêmos* for a citizen in the theatre, is illegal; and this is exactly the kind of award that matters to Goldhill. Demosthenes in his response to Aeschines briefly dismisses what he sees as a legal technicality. He refers somewhat casually to the myriads of citizens to have been honoured with crowns in theatre before (*On the Crown* 120); this exaggerated account conflicts with the lack of clear inscriptional evidence that we have for fourth-century awards of this exact kind.[30] He gives a different account of the laws, in which the people could still vote to have a crown proclaimed in the theatre if they wished. It is unfortunately impossible for us to tell who had the stronger legal case, since the laws themselves do not appear in the texts of these speeches.[31] Aeschines' account of the law may or may not be reliable (he did lose the case); however, he could not have made the argument at all if such a ceremony was a regular occurrence.

One could make the broader observation that the evidence for the ceremonies, whenever they occurred, hints strongly at an atmosphere of democratic ideology and civic pride. It would be an interesting cultural experience to watch plays that 'problematize' the *polis* while attending a festival that otherwise overwhelms the spectator with this atmosphere. But, as we shall see in the next two chapters, the city problematized in tragedy cannot always be identified with Athens; thus the civic ideology of the festival does not find such a direct link with the politics of the plays.

The central difficulty here is the problem of tragedy and democracy. Two issues present themselves: the first is a point to which I shall return in the next chapter, which is that only a minority of the surviving plays represent Athens or any other city as a democracy; second, there is nothing distinctively democratic about the ideology behind Goldhill's four ceremonies, with the possible exception of ceremony number 1, which was performed by elected generals. (And, as we saw in the last chapter, even election was not quite as democratic as appointment by lot.) Number 2 was a demonstration of Athens' imperial power. For Goldhill, number 3 – as in a different way number 4 – demonstrates 'a fundamental and well-known tenet of democratic ideology, namely, that a man acts and should act to benefit the city'.[32] Yet such ideology was a commonplace in Greek political culture more generally. (On the subordination of the individual to the city, and the ways in which this ideology could be tested on the tragic stage, see the discussions of Sophocles' *Ajax* and *Antigone* in ch. 4.)

If there is nothing especially democratic about the four ceremonies, their political significance can be explained in two different ways. First (as Goldhill recognises), they are all in some ways expressions of military might or military ideology. Consequently, with the exception of number 3, which came after the imperial era of the fifth century, they reinforce Athens' importance as the leader of the Delian League. Second, in the case of numbers 4 and (if we can use it) 3, they project a broader political message that was relevant to any Greek city-state.

Both of these points are reinforced by the fact that the surviving tragedies were performed at the City Dionysia and therefore in front of an international audience. As with most issues to do with the theatre audience, we cannot do much more than guess at the numbers of foreign visitors. What we do know is that there were enough of them to be noticed. They were made the more conspicuous by the presence of foreign ambassadors, at least some of them in *prohedriai* (VIP seats);[33] but these dignitaries were not likely to be the only foreign visitors. In the prologue to Aristophanes' comedy *Peace*, performed at the Dionysia of 421 BC, an Athenian audience member is imagined chatting to an Ionian visitor who sits next to him (lines 45–8). *Peace* was produced at the City Dionysia. At the smaller Lenaia festival, it was noticeable that the only foreigners present were the metics: the ones who lived in the city. In Aristophanes' *Acharnians* the leading character, speaking for the poet, says as follows (lines 502–6):

> This time, at least, Cleon cannot allege
> That I have spoken badly of the city
> In front of foreigners. For here we are
> Alone, at the Lenaia. And as yet
> No foreigner is here; for neither has
> The tribute come, nor allies from their cities.

It seems that Cleon had attempted to prosecute Aristophanes for his comedy at the previous year's Dionysia; the play, *Babylonians*, had allegedly presented Athens in a bad light in front of foreigners. Clearly, the foreign component of the audience at the City Dionysia was noticeable in comparison to the Lenaia. Further, these foreigners were enough to make the audience *representative* of other Greek cities. Ambassadors from other members of the Delian League were required to be there, having brought the tribute; and in peace time it seems likely that the festival would have attracted other Greeks too. Even Aeschines, speaking in the fourth century and therefore after the imperial era, could say that the presentation of a crown in the theatre took place 'not in the presence of the people but in the presence of all the Greeks' (*Against Ctesiphon* 34).

There is one further point to be made here. Both Cleon in the fifth century and Aeschines in the fourth are attempting to bring prosecutions against their political enemies, so their bias must be kept in mind; but they will naturally adopt a line of argument that they hope will appeal to an audience of citizens (respectively, the council of 500 and a jury of perhaps about the same number). Crucially, both men adopt a line of argument that says that this kind of display (a comedy that slanders Athens, the award of a crown by the city) is *inappropriate in front of foreigners* (this is the assumption behind Aeschines, *Against Ctesiphon* 33–4). We are left with a distinct sense of self-consciousness. Perhaps not all Athenian politicians would have argued in this way; but it was clearly possible to make an argument before the Athenians that their City Dionysia festival put them on display in front of all of Greece. Perhaps this helps to explain why most tragedies avoid a narrowly democratic perspective.

Rather, the tendency is to reinforce the image Athens would have of itself on an international stage. We know from surviving legal and political speeches that one aspect of this image was as a safe harbour for suppliants and, further, as a city prepared to back up the protection of suppliants with force.[34] This agenda is reflected in the plays themselves, or at least in those that feature the city of Athens.[35] Of around thirty tragedies that survive, only four (*Persians* and *Eumenides* by Aeschylus, *Suppliants* and *Children of Heracles* by Euripides) can be said really to present a democratic Athens in either its institutions or its ideology. (Other plays, set away from Athens, might contain hints of democratic language alongside more universal expressions of *polis* ideology; occasionally they feature democratic assembly meetings.) On the other hand, we have eight tragedies that celebrate Athens as a harbour for suppliants. These are Aeschylus' *Eumenides*, Sophocles' *Oedipus at Colonus*, and the *Medea*, *Children of Heracles*, *Suppliants*, *Heracles*, and (through predictions made in *deus ex machina* speeches) the *Electra* and *Orestes* of Euripides. Among tragedies that have not survived as complete texts we know of at least one, Aeschylus' *Eleusinians*, that also celebrates Athens' protection of suppliants (although in this case through diplomatic, not military means: see Plutarch, *Theseus* 29).

The democratic assumption is highly attractive. It seems plausible to assume that Athenian tragic politics should have more to do with Athenian democracy than anything else. Further, attending the theatrical festivals appears in some way to have been a political act: should not the plays then speak directly to the Athenian citizens who formed the majority of the audience? But the assumption finds little in most of the dramatic evidence to support it. We shall see in the next chapter that the dramatic setting of Greek tragedies tends to reflect the shape of the Greek city-state generally. For the most part, the political slant of the tragedies is similarly general. Where does Athens fit into this? Although Athens features in occasional bursts of celebration, the plays celebrate an idealised foreign policy more often than the democracy itself. More ambiguous references in various plays may reflect an Athenian perspective (see the conclusion to ch. 4), but for the most part the tragic purpose seems to have been to play to a more international audience.

The Brilliant Dynasts

The approach adopted by Goldhill receives substantial qualification from the recent work of Mark Griffith. Griffith has been described as being opposed to the view that tragedy was essentially democratic. In fact, he does make the democratic assumption to this extent: that the tragedies – produced among, by and for the Athenians – must have had relevant things to say for the city of Athens. However, he brings an important qualification to this assumption: the plays negotiate a tension between democratic ideology and elite leadership.[36] There was a difference, in other words, between the ideal Athens, where the people ruled themselves, and the reality of an Athens that relied heavily on the advice and leadership of a small number of citizens, roughly equivalent to the ruling class of other cities. Much contemporary scholarship on tragedy concentrates on ideology; Griffith, to complete the picture, emphasises the role of the elite. The phrase 'Brilliant Dynasts' is the title of one of Griffith's articles, and describes the role in society of the leaders on whom even a democracy depended. It is a literal translation of a phrase (*lamprous dynastas*) from the prologue to Aeschylus' *Agamemnon* (line 6; one notes that the original Greek refers not to people but – metaphorically – to stars in the night sky).

To provide some background, Griffith considers the nature of theatrical performance and some ways in which the original Greek audience might have understood it. He essentially makes two points. The first is that theatre, a medium in which different views and perspectives are given to different characters, is ideally suited to offering more than one perspective at a time, without necessarily saying which one is correct. The second point follows from the first: audience members can adopt multiple perspectives on the action. They can do so, says Griffith, in a simple, physical sense: their viewing is not mediated, like modern TV or cinema audiences, by the shot selection of the director; instead, they observe whom they want, when they want. The audience of Greek tragedy could also adopt several different *sympathetic* perspectives, including the following three:

1. sympathy for the leading characters;

2. the perspective of the gods, looking down on the action from outside, perhaps with a privileged foresight of what will happen next;

3. the perspective of 'lesser' characters: 'along with the fearful choral group or minor character, [the audience] gazes up at these leaders from below with wonder, as stupendously superior pillars of strength, ambition, and determination'.[37]

All three of these perspectives could be adopted more or less at the same time. However, while both the heroes and the gods were so great that the audience could not identify with them, the third perspective allowed audience members (of whatever social position) to identify with more ordinary characters: an often extensive supporting cast including messengers, slaves and chorus members. This third perspective, argues Griffith, was closest to that of the audience since the minor characters and choruses, like the audience members themselves, tend to survive the tragedy and return to their normal lives afterwards.

The third perspective can be illustrated by quotations from the *parodoi* (first choral odes) of two Sophoclean tragedies, *Ajax* (lines 154–61) and *Philoctetes* (135–43):

Strike at a great man, and you will not miss;
But if one should bend such slander at me,
None would believe him. Envy stalks
After magnates of wealth and power;

Yet humble men without their princes
Are a frail prop for a fortress. They
Should be dependent on the great,
And the great should be upheld by lesser ones.

Sir, we are strangers, and this land is strange;
What shall we say and what conceal from this suspicious
    man?
Tell us.
For cunning that passes another's cunning
And a pre-eminent judgement lie with the prince,
In whose sovereign keeping is Zeus's holy sceptre.
To you, young lord, all this has come,
All the power of your forefathers. Tell us now
What we must do to serve you.

Each of these odes, the first sung with Ajax in mind, the second addressed to Neoptolemus, comes from a chorus comprised of the military subordinates of a hero. In both we get a striking picture of the inter-dependence of leader and led. It was possible even for an Athenian to identify with the members of these choruses since the citizens of a democracy were expected to follow orders on the battle-field or on board a warship. The pattern also emerges in non-military passages: a heroic figure – often a political leader – takes risks, makes mistakes and ultimately suffers; lesser characters, who come to represent the city at large, survive. We feel for the hero's suffering just as we are comforted by the survival of the city. Something else survives too: even though the hero-leader himself is frequently doomed, the principle that 'humble men ... Should be dependent on the great, / And the great should be upheld by lesser ones' is reinforced. Our desire for good leadership may be frustrated, but we do not lose this desire. Part of the social function of tragedy, concludes Griffith, is to reinforce the station of the elite in Athenian society.

There are several advantages to Griffith's view. Most importantly, it reflects the political character of the actual plays. Like most or all of the writers discussed on these pages, Griffith starts from the assumption that tragedy was politically relevant to the members of a democracy; but he recognises that it is not always easy to reconcile Athens, a city in which the people were sovereign, with tragedy, a genre in which cities are almost always ruled by kings. (On this problem, see further ch. 3.)

Griffith's view also has a greater relevance to the way in which Athenian democracy actually worked. The guiding principle of this democracy was that the people were always right. In procedural terms, this meant that any proposal for which a majority voted in the assembly was adopted as the city's policy. Proposals, however, did not fall out of the sky: in order to function the assembly relied on the expert advice, expertly given, of the people who addressed it; these speakers were predominantly of the elite.[38] In the fifth century many of these public speakers were also elected as generals. In addition, only a wealthy elite could afford to make the substantial one-off payments, known as *leitourgiai*, on which the city depended. Such payments could finance warships and (as we have seen) dramatic choruses. In many respects it is fair to say that Athens, ideologically run by the masses, was in reality run by the elite in the interests of the masses. A famously disgruntled late fifth-century political pamphleteer, known to modern readership as the Old Oligarch (on whom, see ch. 3), thus hit the mark when he said that 'When it comes to arranging choruses and gymnasia and warships they realise that the rich lead the choruses and the people have choruses led for them; and the rich arrange the gymnasia and the warships and the people have gymnasia and warships arranged for them' (Ps.-Xenophon, *Constitution of the Athenians*, 1.13).

So important parts of Athenian life were arranged by the rich for the benefit of the poor. Further, aspects of Athenian public life took the form of a performance given by elite actors for a mass-elite audience. This was the case in the democratic assembly; it was also the case in the theatre. The theatre audience was far broader in its composition than the body of the assembly, as we saw in ch. 1: it contained foreign visitors, metics, a small number of women and possibly even slaves (though these last two points are contentious); many citizens in addition brought their sons to the tragedies; but the single largest body of people in the audience were still Athenian citizens, both mass and elite. As for the performance, although the poet and the actors were paid at public expense, the chorus was paid for by the *leitourgia* of a rich *chorêgos*. The poets themselves were generally also of elite wealth and standing. In addition, the skill in singing and dancing required to be a chorus member might suggest a level of education not associated with the poorest citizens in classical Athens, although this view has recently been called into question.[39] Broadly, the tragedies, like the debates in the assembly, can be understood as performances put on by the elite for the benefit of all the citizens.

As a further advantage, Griffith fully adopts the kind of audience perspective for which I gave a rationale earlier in this book (pages 6–7, 26–7). However, it is in relating the audience's perspective to the plays that we find difficulties (the only ones that I can see) in Griffith's argument. There are two issues here. First, it is not always clear how ordinary people in the audience could relate to the lesser characters on stage. Griffith's view is that the audience, like the supporting cast of the dramas, was diverse in age, social class and (probably) gender. The problem is that this supporting cast (quite unlike the theatre audience) contains a disproportionately low number of ordinary citizens; further, many of these unnamed figures are not even Greek – they may be foreigners or slaves. Not every non-heroic character in a tragedy is 'just like us'. This is especially true of the choruses in extant tragedy: Griffith himself is quick to point out that few surviving tragedies have choruses of normal citizens as *Ajax* or *Philoctetes* do. Several tragedies have choruses of elders, usually not just old men but members of the political elite. (Two clear exceptions are Euripides' plays *Heracles* and *Children of Heracles*, both of which have elderly-yet-ordinary chorus members.[40]) One answer to this problem is that, even though they do not always appear on stage, the ordinary citizens are present in the background of many political tragedies. I discuss this point fully in the next chapter.

Secondly, the idea that one cannot identify with the heroes of tragedy seems to jar with many other readings, not least that of Aristophanes, for whom the leading characters are supposed to be examples to the citizens. One could can add the general point that it is hard to blame theatre-goers for identifying with whoever happens to be the leading character in the play they are watching. Griffith is certainly correct that many or most tragic protagonists are simply too extraordinary – both in their behaviour and in their fate – to offer useful models for everyday people; but other named characters present more attainable targets (see pages 70–1 below).

Griffith makes the democratic assumption but in a safer way than Goldhill. His views hold just as much relevance for Athenian politics as Goldhill's, while also allowing room for the more generally Greek perspective that I proposed in the last section. His reading also has a much firmer basis in the heroic texts that we have. Athens under democracy was divided by social class like any other Greek city. The heroic pursuit of *timê* (honour, respect), familiar from Homer, found its equivalent in the elite search for personal prestige in the city (see below, pages 100–1). On the other hand, thousands must have embraced the ideology that everyone can rule. It was ultimately up to individual audience members with which tragic figures they identified – and we cannot really know which they chose.

The 'new ritualism'

A rather different way of explaining tragedy in terms of democratic ideology comes from the work of Richard Seaford. For Seaford, most of the tragedies that we have are set not in the world of democracy but of tyranny. We saw in the last chapter that many Greek city-states went through periods of tyranny in the seventh and sixth centuries BC. For the Athenians, the end of tyranny was closely connected with the birth of democracy; the freedom of many other Greek cities, on the other hand, was identified (paradoxically, in the modern view) with oligarchy, the rule of a political elite. Thus Seaford's work is concerned with the formation of the Greek city-state in general. Tragedy, he says, re-enacts this *polis*-formation.

Seaford's work has to do with the role of ritual in tragedy and, closely connected with it in his view, with the god Dionysus. The tragedies were performed at festivals in honour of Dionysus, although the Greeks sometimes doubted the connection between the dramas and the god in whose honour they were supposedly performed – hence the ancient saying that they were 'nothing to do with Dionysus'. Conversely, in modern times the Dionysiac has been a characteristic strain of much criticism of tragedy, in a tradition that goes back to 1872 and Nietzsche's book *The Birth of Tragedy*. Even those modern writers who do not read ritual into the plays tend to accept the view that the origins of tragedy lay in the ritual worship of that god, although this assumption has recently been challenged.[41] Seaford's new perspective on the ritualist reading of tragedy arises from the observation that ritual in tragedy is often distorted or perverted in some way, in contrast to Homeric epic, where ritual is always a source of cohesion and certainty.

Seaford's approach is a model-building one, and his model of political tragedy goes roughly like this. The house of a tyrant suffers a crisis, manifest in the perversion of some ritual. This leads to the self-destruction of the tyrant's *oikos* (household). He either dies or is cast out, to the benefit of the city. A new ritual is then instituted to the benefit thereafter of all the citizens: a *polis*-cult, perhaps a hero-cult in honour of the dead tyrant. In his emphasis on the survival of the city, Seaford shares some common ground with Griffith; but (aside from the ritualism) there are two important differences, one general and the other specific. Griffith's general view is that good leadership emerges from these dramas as desirable; and, in the specific case of Sophocles' *Antigone*, he argues that Creon survives as king at the end.[42]

No tragedy fits Seaford's model perfectly, although some come close in various elements of it. The single play that provides the best fit is probably Euripides' *Bacchae*. Here, the city of Thebes, under the abusive tyrant Pentheus, refuses to celebrate the rites of Dionysus. Pentheus dies in gruesome circumstances, but this at least prevents the punishment of the city that Dionysus has threatened (lines 50–2). The play ends with the foundation of a *polis*-cult in honour of the god Dionysus – at least in Seaford's view.[43] In fact, we cannot be certain that any cult at all is founded here: while Euripides does typically end his plays by giving the mythical origin of a contemporary phenomenon, the part of *Bacchae* in which this might have occurred has not survived. Euripides' *Heracles* also appears to fit quite well, although the hero-cult is associated with the tyrannicide, not the tyrant, and the hero-cult will be located in a different city. In this play the family of Heracles is living in the city of Thebes, which is ruled by a tyrant called Lycus. Lycus has threatened to kill Heracles' children but Heracles returns from his labours and kills the tyrant. He now means to make a sacrifice and cleanse the house, but he is driven mad by the goddess Atê and kills the children himself, a perversion of sacrificial ritual. When Heracles comes to his senses, Theseus arrives from Athens and offers the polluted hero sanctuary. Theseus promises that after his death Heracles will be the object of a hero-cult at the city of Athens (lines 1331–3).

The main advantage of Seaford's approach is that, perhaps even more than any of the approaches we have looked at so far, it takes the historical and cultural context fully into account. Seaford does not merely place the plays in a cultural context; he discusses both the plays and their context simultaneously. For instance (although this is hardly a new observation), the behaviour of various tragic figures when in moods of heightened emotion is identified with that of participants in Dionysiac mysteries. Another advantage, in my view, is the preoccupation with tyranny: by no means all tragedies are set in tyrannies, but this is still an avenue worth exploring – as we shall see from time to time in the next two chapters.

The main advantage of Seaford's approach is also a disadvantage. It leads him to reject purely dramatic concerns in a study of what is, after all, drama. One of his claims is that an inter-disciplinary approach can solve problems in the plays that formalist literary criticism cannot.[44] An example is his consideration of the great 'deception speech' in Sophocles' *Ajax* (lines 646–92; I summarise and discuss this play in ch. 4). Here, Ajax appears to take back his intention to commit suicide, only to kill himself soon afterwards. This speech has puzzled generations of commentators: does this typically intransigent Sophoclean hero really change his mind twice, or is this speech a calculated piece of deception, designed to prevent his family and people from saving him?[45] In the speech, Ajax says (lines 667–8) that he will reconcile himself with his enemies, Agamemnon and Menelaus, and yet he later invokes the Furies against them as he dies (843–4). Does he then mean what he says at 667–8? Seaford's explanation is that this ambiguity foreshadows his dual role as the future subject of hero-cult: both a source of mutual respect and a rallying point for anger against one's enemies. But Sophocles avoids any mention of the cult of Ajax, which is the more remarkable since

Ajax was the subject of a popular hero-cult in the classical period.[46] Further, hero-cults were located at the graves of heroes,[47] yet this play ends with the burial of Ajax on the plain of Troy, far from the location of the historical cult at Salamis or Athens.[48] Seaford's inter-disciplinary instinct is one that he shares with other classical scholars, but here dramatic concerns provide us with a far more satis-fying explanation of both scenes. The deception speech is a typically Sophoclean piece of dramatic ambiguity, wrong-footing the hero's audiences both on stage and in the auditorium. That it is so brilliantly reasoned and composed is an indication of Ajax's greatness and great sensitivity – although not of his intentions.

Seaford is aware of the limitations and variations on his model, saying that 'it seems to apply better to Aeschylus than to Sophokles whose emphasis is generally on the self-destruction [of the tyrant's household] rather than the transition [of the city], or to Euripides, in whose plays the connection between familial self-destruction and eventual *polis*-cult often seems very loose'.[49] This last point deserves a little more elaboration. We have seen that most of Euripides' trag-edies close with an aetiology, a prediction of some future institution deriving from the events of the play. Frequently this aetiology predicts a religious cult, either of a god or a hero. To predict a cult, however, is not the same thing as to found it: Euripides' concern seems to be more with aetiology than with the foundation of cult for its own sake.[50]

Seaford's model works particularly badly for the surviving plays of Sophocles, in two respects. First, only in *Oedipus at Colonus* is there a clear reference to a future hero-cult – and even this is problematic, since it is unclear where a historical cult of Oedipus would have been situated.[51] This matters, since a hero-cult was located at the grave of the hero. If nobody knew where this was, there could be no cult.[52] In the play, details of the tomb's location are carefully left vague: only Theseus knows where it is and he is sworn to secrecy. The idea is that the secret will be transmitted through perpetuity from dying father to first-born son, so that at any one time there is only one man alive who knows it (see lines, 1522–32, and compare 1760–3). This, however, seems difficult to reconcile with the traditional story of Theseus' death: thrown treacherously off a cliff on the island of Scyros. The original audience of Sophocles' play, it seems, was not asked to assume that this secret survived even one generation.

It can be (and has been) argued that Sophocles' *Ajax*, *Women of Trachis* and *Philoctetes* look forward implicitly to different hero-cults.[53] I discussed *Ajax* above. *Women of Trachis* ends as Heracles is being taken away to be placed alive on a pyre on Mt Oeta, the location of a cult of Heracles in the classical period. This event is more consistent with Heracles' status as an immortal god (having been rescued from the pyre by Athene and taken to Olympus) than with the less frequent tradition of the dead hero.[54] As for *Philoctetes*, it has been suggested that the following lines, spoken by Heracles as *deus ex machina*, look forward to the cult worship of Philoctetes in southern Italy[55] (Sophocles, *Philoctetes* 1418–22):

> Let me reveal to you my own story first,
> Let me show the tasks and sufferings that were mine,
> And, at the last, the winning of deathless merit.
> All this you see in me now.
> All this must be your suffering too,
> The winning of a life to an end in glory,
> Out of this suffering.

But these words more plausibly refer to the immortal, heroic *fame* that Philoctetes will win once he is transported to Troy.

Secondly, and more politically, where a Sophoclean tyrant is driven out or ruined, it is never clear how this will benefit the city. Sophocles' *Electra*, a version of the killing of Clytemnestra and Aegisthus, has been read as a positive account of tyrant-killing with corresponding benefits for the house of Atreus and the city of Argos; however, it can just as easily be seen as a profoundly unsettling play in which the future of the tyrannicides is left in the balance.[56] There are two other possible examples of deposed tyrants in extant Sophocles: Oedipus in *Oedipus the King* and Creon in *Antigone*. The expulsion of Oedipus from Thebes ought (according to the Delphic oracle) to relieve the city of a dreadful plague. However, Oedipus has not been driven out by the end of *Oedipus the King*, and in fact the plague goes unmentioned in the closing scenes of the play. Further, Oedipus cannot be described as a tyrant since – as he himself finds out – his father was the previous king.[57] At the end of *Antigone* Creon may have lost his family and his reputation, but (as Mark Griffith reminds us) there is no indication that he has been deposed as king. (On *Oedipus the King*, see further ch. 3; on Creon's possible status as tyrant in *Antigone*, ch. 4.)

Seaford's views on political tragedy are informed by a particular type of ritualism. In other words, he seeks to explain events on the dramatic stage in terms of ritual. While this reflects an important and pervasive aspect of ancient Greek life, Seaford's application of ritual, alongside other aspects of his model, is rather too restrictive to work.

Tragedy and the others

An important and comparatively recent strand of scholarship on ancient Greece has constructed a series of binary oppositions between the Greeks and various 'others'. Such oppositions are Greek / barbarian, free / slave, male / female, and even mortal / immortal. These oppositions do not merely follow a modern structuralist scheme: it seems that the Greeks thought of themselves in these terms. Concepts such as slavery (un-freedom) and barbarism (un-Greekness) tended to reinforce the Greek self-image. To be a citizen of Athens one had to be adult, free, male and of Athenian descent. The vast majority of modern books on classical Athens have been written about people who met these criteria. The social historian might be just as interested in the life led by the child, the slave, the woman, the non-Athenian or indeed the non-Greek. As most or all of our literary evidence comes from free men, this kind of history is hard to write. An easier, equally interesting question to answer is: how did these free men write about the others?

Drama is of special interest to this kind of study since the (male Athenian) dramatists could give these others a presence and a voice on the tragic or comic stage. In addition, the joint study of Greeks and others gives breadth to the study of politics and tragedy. It provides necessary breadth to a political study since, although a Greek city in constitutional terms was quite literally its citizens, it comprised many more groups of people and relied on them to function socially and economically. It provides necessary breadth to the study of tragedy since even the most political plays rarely have casts consisting exclusively of free Greek males. (In fact, only one such work survives: Sophocles' *Philoctetes*.)

A recent examination of Greeks and others in tragedy comes from Edith Hall. Hall identifies several recurrent patterns in Greek tragedy that reinforce the Greek idea of their own society. Drawing on the opposition of citizen / non-citizen, she observes that in many tragedies the leading characters have been displaced or exiled, and so do not enjoy the legal protection and social privileges enjoyed by members of a *polis*. An example is Sophocles' *Women of Trachis*, where Heracles and his wife Deianeira are living as foreigners at Trachis. We can also consider any of the various tragedies in which Orestes has been exiled from Argos. Looking at the opposition of man / woman, Hall observes that crises in tragedy are frequently caused by women, but only when they are temporarily or permanently without husbands. Deianeira can again be taken as an example:

she unintentionally kills her husband by sending him poison that she thought was a love potion; this comes at the end of a period of fifteen months spent without Heracles. By portraying a person who is without a city, or a woman who is without a legal guardian, tragedy can underline the virtue of living in a stable *oikos* within a stable *polis*: in many ways, as we shall see in the next chapter, this is the most genuinely Greek way in which tragedy can be political.

Tragedy also gives these various others a public voice. For instance, Medea can complain eloquently about the life of a woman in Euripides' play (lines 230–51). Hall is aware of the obvious limitations of this as evidence: these others were played by male citizen actors, speaking lines written by male citizen poets, for a predominantly male citizen audience.[58] There is nothing remotely authentic about what they say, any more than there is in a scene from Aristophanes' *Frogs* (738 ff.), in which two slaves swap anecdotes about the tricks they like to play on their masters. But we can take an interest in how their words *sound* authentic to the intended audience and in whether this tells us anything about the audience's view of women, slaves or foreigners.

This approach is important and not to be neglected by anyone seriously interested in the politics of tragedy. It adds breadth to our study, but arguably too much breadth. We have come as far as it is possible to come from Podlecki's historicist conception of the political. This problem of breadth (which I address in the next chapter) was raised above in the context of Macleod's idea of community. To be fair, Hall does not claim to address questions of tragic politics directly. Instead she focuses on what she calls the 'sociology' of tragedy while showing its relevance to Athenian democracy. This all serves to reinforce the point that in any study of the politics of Greek tragedy one must have a coherent idea of the word 'political'. Most of the differences between the approaches I have described in this chapter can be reduced to different definitions of that word. In the next chapter I offer a working definition of the political for the purposes of the rest of this book.

The *Oresteia*: a multiplicity of political readings

All of the political readings outlined in this chapter can be applied to a greater or lesser extent in Aeschylus' Oresteian trilogy, which I discussed briefly above. Here is a longer summary of the plot of the trilogy, interspersed with some political observations.

In the prologue of *Agamemnon*, a watchman observes the lighting of a distant beacon, the end of a chain of fire signals that announces the fall of Troy to the Greeks. The chorus of Argive elders enters and delivers the *parodos* (lines 40–257). They remember the events of ten years before, when the Greek fleet set off for Troy. The goddess Artemis was preventing the wind that the fleet needed to sail until Agamemnon sacrificed his own daughter Iphigenia. Agamemnon did this terrible thing. As part of the *parodos*, the chorus express their faith in the justice of the universe, wisely led by Zeus (160–83). Given that there is justice, Agamemnon may face dire consequences on his return home. Macleod, as we have seen, points out that issues of justice will be explored throughout the trilogy.

The first person to return from Troy (at line 489) is a herald from the Greek army. Following a further choral ode (681–781), Agamemnon himself returns. The enthusiasm with which the chorus welcomes him, Griffith points out, is a reflection of the extent to which they value aristocratic leadership (782–9, quoted below on page 85). This is the famous scene in which Clytemnestra has some slaves create a makeshift carpet made from fine clothing materials – red tapestries taken from around the house – and persuades Agamemnon to enter the house by walking on it. Clytemnestra's welcome (from line 855) will later seem dishonest, given her intentions and given that she has been carrying on an affair with Agamemnon's cousin Aegisthus. She gives an honest account in some details, however: for example, where she says that she has sent their son Orestes away to the court of Strophius, king of Phocis. This, argues Griffith, exploits the ties of *xenia* (guest-friendship) that existed internationally between aristocratic houses.

Agamemnon enters the house, at which point the scene might be expected to end; but the audience will have noticed that he did not come back alone. With him is Cassandra, daughter of Priam, king of Troy. The story goes that the god Apollo was infatuated with her but she refused him; Apollo then cursed Cassandra so that she would have the gift of prophecy but nobody would ever believe her. Cassandra knows that she and Agamemnon are about to die but she can do nothing about it. She sings at length (from line 1072) about her predicament, on which Hall elaborates: she is a female member of a barbarian royal house who has suffered the great reversal of being made a slave. This eccentric yet sympathetic character is thus one of the 'others' on three counts. Following a long dialogue with the chorus, Cassandra enters the house.

In a stunning tableau to echo and rival that of the red tapestries, we are presented with the dead bodies of Agamemnon and Cassandra, over whom stands the bloodstained and triumphant Clytemnestra. The chorus censure and threaten her but she asserts the justice of her deed (1372–1577). Aegisthus enters and (from line 1578) celebrates this act of vengeance-justice with reference to another past deed. Aegisthus' father Thyestes had had an affair with the wife of his brother Atreus, who was the father of Agamemnon. In response to this, Atreus had killed Aegisthus' two elder brothers and served them up to the unknowing Thyestes. As far as Aegisthus is concerned, the killing of Agamemnon is righteous punishment for his father's crime. Again, as Macleod and others would remind us, our ideas of justice are being tested.

Libation Bearers begins seven years later with the return of Orestes, now a young man, in disguise. He is accompanied by Pylades, son of Strophius. Orestes is reunited with his sister Electra and then, following the command of the Delphic oracle, kills his mother in revenge for his father. He hesitates on the point of committing this dreadful act but Pylades (in his only speech of the play, lines 900–2) urges him to proceed. Griffith again underlines the importance of aristocratic ties of *xenia*, such as exist between these two young men, to the outcome of the drama.[59] Clytemnestra has all this time been living with Aegisthus and appears to be the senior partner in the affair. This is an ongoing perversion of marriage ritual, which Seaford would see as indicative of the problems in this royal house. Hence Orestes complains that the citizens of Argos, conquerors of Troy, 'go subject to this brace of women' (lines 302–4).

Following the matricide, Orestes is pursued from the stage by the Furies, dread goddesses of blood-guilt, whom only he can see. The Furies, euphemistically known as Eumenides ('well-disposed ones') are the chorus of the third play, to which they give their name and in which they are visible to the audience. They chase Orestes first to Delphi and then to Athens. Here he calls on the city's patron goddess, Athene, to come to his aid (276–98). Although the Furies stake their claim to drive the killer to misery, they agree that he can stand trial on the Areopagus first, no doubt confident that they will win their case (415–35). The Eumenides lead the prosecution, Apollo speaks for Orestes, and Athene herself is president of this, the first ever homicide court. This court will establish a judicial solution to the blood feud that has blighted the house of Atreus for generations. Thus the questions of justice, raised in the trilogy and underlined by Macleod, reach a conclusion.

The establishment of this court is significant for historicists, too. The court in question is not the usual democratic law-court; it is the Areopagus council, an ancient body that sat on the rocky hill of that name (Areopagus means 'the crag of Ares'). This was the ancient aristocratic council of Athens and it had kept many of its powers after the reforms of Cleisthenes in 508/7 BC. However, we saw in ch. 1 that the ability of the Areopagus council to rival the democratic assembly came to an end in 462/1, not long before the *Oresteia* was performed: its role was reduced to that of a homicide court. It seems unclear whether, by portraying the Areopagus council as a homicide court and nothing else, Aeschylus is underlining and promoting its new role, or whether he is advancing its ancient claims to real power in the most subtle way available (or, as Macleod argues, neither of the above).

Podlecki provides good grounds for believing that Aeschylus is taking a radically democratic line, even though he is promoting an ancient aristocratic council. The man behind the reform of the Areopagus was Ephialtes. In 461 Ephialtes diminished the influence of his less radical rival Cimon by successfully proposing the Argive alliance. Cimon had close ties with Sparta, historically an enemy of Argos. With the Argive alliance Ephialtes managed simultaneously to damage the political standing of Cimon and to distance Athens from the oligarchic form of government favoured by the Spartans. There are three clear, positive references to the alliance in *Eumenides*. When he first invokes Athena, Orestes, heir to the throne of Argos, promises undying and unconditional loyalty to Athens (289–91). Apollo makes a similar promise in anticipation of Orestes' acquittal (669–73). Upon receiving the verdict, Orestes repeats his promise along with one of a non-aggression pact between Argos and Athens (762–74). If Aeschylus is supporting Ephialtes on the Argive alliance, says Podlecki, then he is adding his support on the reform of the Areopagus too.

For all the apparent radical democratic loyalties of its author, Griffith also detects a possible reference to the value of aristocratic ties of *xenia*. When Orestes first identifies himself to Athene, a goddess he now knows will preside over his trial, he points out that she and his father fought together in the Trojan War (455–8).

Athene assembles a court of Athenian citizens. Apollo and the Furies respectively lead the defence and prosecution. Asked for a verdict, the jury is split down the middle. Orestes is acquitted on Athene's casting vote (752–3). The Furies are outraged. Athene appeases them (starting at line 848) by offering them a new role: they will live perpetually under the Areopagus as guardians of this new model of justice. These Furies were the object of a religious cult in the city of Athens, so that the end of this trilogy provides a reasonably good fit with Seaford's model. The promotion of the democratic city in this play is also important to Goldhill's thesis. Goldhill considers the following speech (696–703):

> No anarchy, no rule of a single master. Thus
> I advise my citizens to govern and to grace,
> And not to cast fear utterly from your city. What
> Man who fears nothing at all is ever righteous? Such
> Be your just terrors, and you may deserve and have
> Salvation for your citadel, your land's defence,
> Such as is nowhere else found among men, neither
> Among the Scythians, nor the land that Pelops held.

Democracy, Goldhill points out, is presented as a middle way between anarchy and tyranny. While the citizens of democracy enjoy freedom and self-governance, they also have a healthy fear of the law and of the authority of the city.[60]

Which reading is the correct one? All of them seem valuable. If the *Oresteia* satisfies most of the available readings, that is perhaps because many modern political readings of Greek tragedy have been formulated with the *Oresteia* chiefly in mind. It is also because Aeschylus in the *Oresteia* is weaving one of the richest tapestries in Greek literature. As one aspect of this richness, the *Oresteia* is an unusually political piece of work even by the standards of Greek tragedy. The final part of the trilogy reaches a height of enthusiasm for Athenian democracy that most other tragedies do not match, including some of the other ones set in Athens. Nor are historical references made as clear in most other tragedies.

As regards other Greek tragedies, some political readings are more useful than others. One conclusion to be drawn from this chapter is that to search for a single, unifying theory of the politics of Greek tragedy is hopeless. Some tragedies are more political than others and some are hardly political at all. Different plays are political in different ways. That said, it is worth our while to search for a 'best fit' definition of the political in tragedy. It is to this search that we now turn.

CHAPTER 3

THE POLITICAL
SHAPE OF TRAGEDY

Problem: what do we mean by 'political'?

There are two lessons to be drawn from the survey in the previous chapter: first, that different tragedies are political in different ways and second, that any inquiry into the politics of Greek tragedy must be informed by a working definition of the 'political'. Disregarding for the moment the need for flexibility necessitated by my first point, I attempt to find such a definition here.

A good starting point is Macleod's definition of the political as 'a concern with human beings as part of a community'. This has a special relevance to the study of ancient Greece. The life of the Greek city-state brought with it a great sense of *koinônia* (community); the degree to which this was the case would seem surprising to a visitor from a nation state, especially one used to the sharply individualist culture of the modern West. When Aristotle famously wrote that 'man is by nature a political animal' (a *politikon zôon*), he did not mean the modern sense of the word 'political' so much as he meant that man is an animal whose natural habitat is the community of the *polis*.[61] We get an idea of this sense of community from one of the key surviving texts on Athenian democratic ideology. At the end of each year of a war a leading citizen gave an address in honour of the war dead. In 430, at the end of the first year of the Peloponnesian War, this honour fell to Pericles. Thucydides records what purport to be Pericles' words. The following extract is from Thucydides 2.40:

> Here [at Athens] each individual is interested not only in his own affairs but in the affairs of the state as well: even those who are mostly occupied in their own business are extremely well-informed on general politics – this is a peculiarity of ours: we do not say that a man who takes no interest in politics is a man who minds his own business; we say that he has no business here at all.

This is a wartime speech and it suits Pericles' purpose to emphasise the 'peculiarity' of Athenian democracy in comparison with rival Greek cities. It is striking nevertheless that he makes a virtue of political engagement as a social obligation in the context of what, by Greek standards, was a liberal society. (Elsewhere in the speech he praises non-interference in *private* life as an Athenian virtue: Thucydides 2.37, quoted below on page 96.) In fact, Athens was only the most extreme example of Greek *koinônia*, since all its (free, male) citizens were politically enfranchised.

So the Greek idea of community could be a highly politicised one. This begins to get around the problem of breadth in Macleod's definition that I raised in the last chapter; for if the dominant idea of community was of the *polis*, a public community of citizens and laws, then a 'concern with community' must be a political concern, not just a sociological one. (Within the Athenian *polis*, even local communities were organised into political units called demes.) But there is a further problem with breadth. If we remember that not all human beings were (male) citizens, then a concern with the community is with not just free men but with women, children, slaves and metics. There are at least as many significant women in tragedy as men, and more than a few slaves in various roles. Is a tragedy that features women more than men a less political play? Crudely, the answer from a Greek point of view is yes; but we can approach the question in a more sophisticated way.

The *oikos* (household) was the basic political unit, one of the building blocks of the *polis*. (This set of priorities is reflected in Aristotle in the *Politics*: he devotes most of book 1 to a discussion of household management.) The conceptual difference between these two institutions (in Athens at any rate) can be explained in three ways. First, the *oikos* was a mini-community of men, women and children, slave and free, with a male citizen at its head.[62] The Greek word for the head of a household, the legal guardian of its members, was the *kurios*. Each *kurios* was also a *politês* – a member of the *polis*, a citizen. The *polis*, in contrast to the *oikos*, was a community of free adult males. Second, the *oikos* was a more private world. The citizen women in the household (his wife and daughters, and other relatives) ideally lived their lives inside and in private; the exceptions were religious festivals, where women could play at least as important a public role as men. An Athenian man was only likely to enter another man's house if he was a close relative or if he had the owner's explicit permission; it was especially shameful to be in the same room as another man's wife.[63] Third, while the life of the *oikos* was contained indoors, the business of the *polis* was conducted for the most part in the open air. Therefore one can increase one's understanding of classical Athens if one constructs a close correlation between each of the following sets of oppositions: *oikos* / *polis*, private / public, indoors / outdoors and (to some extent) female / male. Further, it is possible to draw a dichotomy between the citizen's domestic role and his political role; between a private interaction with members of his own family and a public interaction with other citizens. The former went on indoors; the latter took place in the assembly, the council house, the law courts and the *agora* (a combined market and meeting place) – predominantly in the open air.

A tragedy can thus be said to be more political the more its male characters are engaged in the public life of the city. And even tragic women can be politicised if they become embroiled in public affairs: this is the case in Sophocles' *Antigone*, a play discussed in the next chapter. However, it does not necessarily follow that a tragedy is less political if it dramatises the affairs of an *oikos*. Political tragedies tend to be concerned with the *oikos* and the *polis* simultaneously: an example is Aeschylus' *Libation Bearers*, where the killing of Aegisthus and Clytemnestra rids both the city of tyrants and the house of adulterers. The scene of the typical tragedy is simultaneously public and private: generally tragedies are set quite literally on the doorstep, where *oikos* meets *polis*. Some tragedies, however, focus outwards on the *polis* less than others. For instance, in both Sophocles' and Euripides' versions of the story told in *Libation Bearers*, more attention is paid to the character of Electra, Orestes' sister, who gives her name to both plays. These dramas are in different ways less concerned with the affairs of the city than *Libation Bearers*, a drama in whose second half Electra plays no part.[64] We might therefore extend Macleod's definition of the political and arrive at the following: *a concern with human beings as part of the community of the polis.*

More generally, the level of political, as opposed to (concurrently) domestic, interest in tragedy can vary. The number of significant male characters can be a rough index of this variation, as is the gender of the chorus. The seven extant tragedies of Sophocles will provide some illustration of this point. The three 'Theban' plays are so called because they each draw on the myth of the royal house of Thebes. Although they were not conceived as a trilogy, individually they are highly political plays (of these, I consider *Antigone* at length in the next chapter, *Oedipus the King* and *Oedipus at Colonus* briefly in this one). The protagonists of the Theban plays are kings or former kings and the chorus members are elders. (Of course a woman is one of the principal characters in *Antigone* – the other is

Creon – but the play after its prologue is male drama, into which women intrude.) In two other Sophoclean plays we have a chorus of women: *Electra*, we have observed, is less preoccupied with the city than it might be; *Women of Trachis* is not really a political drama. As implied in the title, the chorus members of *Women of Trachis* are representatives of the local community; but we get no real sense of a city of Trachis apart from a brief reported scene from the market place. In the other two plays the chorus is one of soldiers or sailors: the military here can be taken as an extension of the political, since citizens could be expected to fight or row for their city in time of war (see further the discussion of *Ajax* in the next chapter). Of these two, *Ajax* has a domestic aspect, although the 'family' is a spear-won, servile family at a military camp and the house is a tent; *Philoctetes* has an entirely male cast.

The definition I have given (a concern with human beings as part of the community of the *polis*) will do broadly, it is hoped, for all the plays. However, we can add greater complexity to the picture. Different tragedies are political in different ways, three of which we shall consider in the next few pages. One aspect of the political in tragedy has to do with the exercise of political power. In a purely domestic tragedy, any power issue is uncontroversial: the head of the household is in charge. Wives (like Clytemnestra in *Agamemnon*) may exercise a kind of surreptitious control over their husbands; sons (like Haemon in *Antigone*) may defy their fathers' authority; but these characters only serve to transgress a domestic norm. Issues of power can be made more complicated on the political stage than in a domestic context, as I hope will become apparent in some of the discussions that follow.

A good example of such complication is Euripides' *Iphigenia at Aulis*.[65] This play dramatises the events leading up to Agamemnon's sacrifice of his daughter to Artemis. Agamemnon (it will be remembered from the discussion in the last chapter of Aeschylus' play) will not have the wind the Greek fleet needs for the voyage to Troy unless he sacrifices his daughter Iphigenia to the goddess Artemis. Iphigenia, accompanied by her mother Clytemnestra and the baby Orestes, is summoned to Aulis, where the Greek fleet is moored, on the pretext that she is to be married to the Greek hero Achilles. Behind the drama lies a tension between the violent potential of an army, eager and impatient for war, and the supposed authority of its generals. Agamemnon is characterised, rather as he is in Homer's *Iliad*, as an indecisive man who is not quite able to deal with the responsibility thrust upon him. In the prologue to *Iphigenia at Aulis* he says that he envies 'men who without peril / Pass through their lives, obscure, / Unknown' (lines 17–18). His brother Menelaus, for the sake of whose marriage the war will be fought, seems to have an unreasonably strong influence over him, affecting his judgement. Achilles, to whom both the supposed marriage and the actual sacrifice come as a bitter surprise, tries unsuccessfully to persuade the army against the sacrifice. Odysseus, whom we do not see, is spoken of as an unscrupulous and devious figure who will rouse the army against Agamemnon if the fleet does not sail (522–35, 1361–6).[66] The play has its domestic aspect, to be sure: the killing of his own daughter will have disastrous consequences for Agamemnon's own marriage and household. In addition, the final decision that allows the sacrifice of Iphigenia to go ahead is made by the young woman herself. Yet the composition of much of the play, as a dialogue between powerful men, makes this a political drama in the purest modern sense of that word. The political situation is unusual in various ways: as in the *Iliad*, each of the heroes is king in his own community and therefore has a sense of his own political prestige; the drama is set in a military camp far from the city, yet the domestic life of Agamemnon intrudes into this camp in the shape of his wife and daughter. That said, many other tragedies, populated by kings, are similarly interested in issues of political or military leadership.

We saw a second aspect of the political in tragedy in the discussion of the *Oresteia* (ch. 2): tragedies can be preoccupied with issues of justice. These issues are the province of Zeus throughout the trilogy; they become fully politicised in *Eumenides* when the judicial authority of a court of law comes into play. Justice in this way comes under the control of the *polis*. This political idea of justice rests on the rule of law, an important idea to the Greeks, which is examined in several surviving tragedies (see for example the discussion of Sophocles' *Antigone* in the next chapter).

Thirdly, tragedies can concern themselves with the life of the *polis* on a more personal level for its original audience members. Specifically, tragedy was understood to teach its audience to be good citizens, to be good members of the *polis*. This is certainly an authentically Greek view – the premise behind the second half of Aristophanes' *Frogs* – but there are two difficulties that we have to face before we can accept this as an idea of *political* tragedy. The first difficulty is that there seem to be remarkably few characters in tragedy who present examples of ordinary Greek citizenship. For one thing, most of the free-born men in tragedy are kings and princes. For another, tragic heroes are correspondingly heroic and elevated in character; and they frequently do or suffer dreadful acts (compare the view of Mark Griffith, discussed in the last chapter). If there are lessons to be learned from tragic heroes, they often come from *not* following their example. This tends to be the case in a Sophoclean tragedy where a great and stubborn hero fails to learn the vital social characteristic of *sôphrosynê* (moderate good sense). As for the minor (unnamed) characters and the choruses, many of them are too different in status from the Greek citizen to serve as an example (see pages 48–9 above). We are frequently left, perhaps, with the example set by some of the secondary characters whose role is help or support the hero: consider for example Odysseus in Sophocles' *Ajax*, discussed in the next chapter.[67] Next to these thoughts, however, should be placed the warning – given elsewhere in this book – against trying too hard to reconstruct the response of individuals in an ancient audience.

The second difficulty with the tragedy-as-example reading is that it does not only explain *political* tragedy. A positive or negative example of a citizen on stage can just as easily be an example of a husband or father as a citizen. It is a reminder that any attempt to separate the domestic and the political in tragedy must be artificial.

One occasional preoccupation of tragedy has to do not with citizen behaviour but with the more fundamental question of citizen status. The importance of this was clear to the Athenians, who in the year 451 voted to restrict citizenship to men descended from Athenians on both sides of the family. To be entered onto his local deme register (and therefore become a citizen) an eighteen-year-old Athenian had to attend a public meeting in which the legitimacy of his birth was established. Other Greek cities guarded citizenship equally jealously. In Sparta a boy went through years of training in order to become a Spartan warrior; but in order finally to achieve this status he had as a young man to be accepted into a kind of soldiers' mess called a *syssition* (and, thereafter, to maintain his contributions to this common mess). If no *syssition* would accept him (and it only took one member to 'black ball' an application), he could not gain the status of a Spartiate.[68] So in their very different ways the Athenians and Spartans required their young men to be accepted formally into the community. Greek cities did not tend to extend citizenship lightly to their own sons, let alone men born outside.

Citizen status – certainly at Athens – gave a man the ability to speak freely in public life. In Euripides' tragedy *Ion* the title character has been brought up away from Athens, although his mother is an Athenian. Unaware of his birth, he worries aloud (671–5):

And she who bore me – may she be a woman
Of Athens, so to give me *parrhêsia*
Inherited on my mother's side. For if
Some foreigner should land inside a city
Of pure blood, while in word he may be called
A citizen, in fact the mouth he gets
Is just a slave; he has no *parrhêsia*.

It is interesting that good parentage is associated here with the lack of restrictions on *parrhêsia* (a tendency – particularly associated with the Athenians – to say what one likes: see ch. 1).[69] In Sophocles' *Ajax* (as we shall see in the next chapter) Agamemnon questions Teucer's ability to speak freely in front of the Greek generals at Troy, on the grounds that Teucer's mother was a slave.

The importance of having the right parents is rather more complicated in Sophocles' *Oedipus the King*, to which I shall be referring frequently in the next few pages and which I summarise now. This is the play in which Oedipus finds out that he has killed his father and married his mother, with whom he has had several children. At the beginning of the action he believes, as he has always done, that his parents are the king and queen of Corinth. He became king of Thebes after he saved that city from a monster called the Sphinx. He also married Jocasta, widow of Laius, who previously ruled Thebes. Thebes is now afflicted with a plague. Oedipus' brother-in-law Creon reports from the Delphic oracle that Laius' killer is still at large in the city and that the plague will go away when the regicide is driven out. Oedipus' investigations lead first Jocasta and then Oedipus to the horrible truth. She commits suicide and he blinds himself in shame.

So Oedipus begins the play under the impression that he is an immigrant ruler who has been adopted as king. Again, a link is made between citizenship and free speech: he makes a public speech, as he puts it, 'citizen to citizens' (line 222). When he is later revealed not to be the son of the king of Corinth his standing is thrown into doubt. Jocasta runs inside with the intention of killing herself, having already realised the dreadful truth; but Oedipus assumes that she is ashamed to have married someone of possibly low birth (1076–85). His marriage until this point might have been understood as an aristocratic alliance between members of different cities (of a kind made impossible in Athens after 451). Ironically, his status as a Theban by birth will be his undoing.

The place of the city in tragedy

If political tragedy is concerned with the community of the *polis*, then it is interesting to see what place the *polis* has in Greek tragedy. I want to consider this in the next two sections, before moving on to a further problem of political tragedy. It will be seen that in its very structure Greek tragedy is concerned closely with the Greek city-state. The *polis* can be defined both as a physical space and as the sum of its citizens. This section considers the representation of the *polis* as a physical space in tragedy; in the next section, we shall consider how tragedy represents the citizen body of a city.[70] I refer in these two sections to several dramas, making special reference to Sophocles' *Oedipus the King*. This tragedy serves as a good example for many of the points I want to make.

An important strand of recent scholarship on Greek tragedy has been concerned with the use of dramatic space in tragedy. Such works look at the ways in which the original productions might have used the performance space of the Theatre of Dionysus; they are also concerned with the picture built up in the audience's mind of what goes on off stage, in what is often called 'reported space'. The achievement of these modern works has been to reignite interest in the plays as works for the stage and to throw emphasis on the

Greek theatre as a visual medium, not just a verbal one. It is my contention here that, in two very simple and fundamental ways, the use of tragic space reflects the popular political assumptions of the ancient Greeks. We can find tragedy to be political in its very structure, before we even look at its meaning.[71]

The first sense in which tragic space reflects political assumptions has to do the place of the *oikos* within the *polis*.[72] We have seen that the *oikos* was a building block of the *polis*, and that the indoor, private world of the one stood in relation to the outdoor, public spaces of the city. From at the latest 458 BC tragic playwrights were able to make much of this series of dichotomies. It was probably around this time that a building was constructed at the back of the stage. The evidence for this is the dramas themselves: plays up until that point make no use of a stage building; plays afterwards use it extensively. The earliest surviving drama to have used this piece of scenery – to great effect – is Aeschylus' Oresteian trilogy, first produced in 458.[73] Post-Aeschylean tragedies are likewise set in front of some building or other, typically the house of a major character but sometimes a shrine or some other building. Characters could enter and leave the stage through a door in the middle of the building; messengers could report what went on inside; but the stage action took place immediately *outside*. Occasionally, the action represents what would normally have taken place within, frequently between two female members of the same household. The conversation between two sisters that forms the prologue of Sophocles' *Antigone* ought to take place indoors, but Antigone explains to Ismene that she has brought them outside so that they will not be overheard. When the ailing Phaedra first appears on stage in Euripides' *Hippolytus*, the nurse explains that she had begged to be in the open air. It appears in these two examples (and others) that the poet has contrived a reason for characters to come outside who normally would not.

The audience is, in fact, being allowed to eavesdrop on purely domestic affairs.

It is usually the case, however, that what takes place outside is supposed to take place outside, in public space. It is common for a tragedy to be set in front of a palace or private house, which in turn is located in a city. Anybody entering from the stage building in such a play is proceeding directly from private to public space. The first entry of Medea in Euripides' play of that name could possibly be one of the contrived female entrances that I describe above; but she stays outside for much of the rest of the drama, conversing with several male characters including two kings. It has been observed that in this entrance she moves deliberately and irreversibly from domestic into political space – a move she describes in her first words not to be spoken from inside: 'Women of Corinth, I have left the house' (line 214).[74] In the prologue of *Oedipus the King*, the plague-ridden Thebans gather before Oedipus' palace to ask for his help. Oedipus comes out to meet them. His brother-in-law Creon has gone to the oracle at Delphi to ask the advice of Apollo. When Creon appears, he expects to relate Apollo's advice to Oedipus in private, within the house. Oedipus insists that the news is heard in public, where everyone can hear (lines 91–4).

So any tragedy that is located before a house in a city is political to this extent: its staging negotiates the boundary between the private and the public lives of citizens. However, such tragedies often create a second dichotomy, which exists between this civilized *oikos-polis* nexus on the one hand and the outside world on the other. If the boundary between *oikos* and *polis* is represented by the door of the stage building, the route to this outside world is represented by one or both of the *eisodoi*, the entrances at either side of the performance space. This outside world can contain other *poleis* – in *Oedipus the King*, Creon enters from Delphi and a messenger later arrives from Corinth – but it can also represent areas that fall outside the civilizing influence of the city. Two such areas are referred to in *Oedipus the King*: one is the place where three roads meet, the site of Oedipus' killing of his father many years previously; the other is Mt Cithaeron, where Oedipus was supposed to have been exposed as a baby years before that. Both areas are represented as outside the authority of any city: the road junction lies between the cities of Thebes, Delphi and Daulia; the mountain is uninhabited in the winter but available for shepherds from both Thebes and Corinth to graze their flocks in the summer (see lines 1132–40). Many tragedies that are set in cities come with a similar sense of a wilder outside world. Mt Cithaeron features again in Euripides' *Bacchae*. Here the mountain is a wild place onto which the maddened women of the city are driven, letting their hair down, suckling wild animals and committing acts of superhuman violence. Hence, when these women – normally confined to the private areas of the city – act savagely, they do so outside its walls as well as its authority. Tragedies in which the city is, has been or will be under attack can come with a sense of a no man's land just outside the walls: one thinks of Thebes, under siege in Aeschylus' *Seven Against Thebes*, Sophocles' *Antigone* or Euripides' *Phoenician Women*; there are other examples. Places outside the walls of a city, therefore, are frequently considered to be outside its authority.

There are, however, degrees of authority cast on rural spaces. For example, Euripides' *Electra* takes place where the title character now lives, on the edge of the territory of Argos. This allows the exiled Orestes to slip in with ease and plan his revenge on the killers of Agamemnon; but this district still comes under the authority of Aegisthus and Clytemnestra. One of the most striking demonstrations of the civilising influence of the city in tragedy is Sophocles' *Philoctetes* (which I discussed briefly in ch. 2). This play is set on a deserted shore on the island of Lemnos, far away from any *polis*. The stage building represents not the title character's house, but his cave. The lack of civilization, the extent to which the world of the *polis* is missed, is apparent throughout.[75] This uninhabited Lemnos is in itself something of a departure from literary tradition. Although the Philoctetes plays of Aeschylus and Euripides have not survived, we know from another ancient source (Dio Chrysostom 52) that these two plays had choruses made up of people from the island.

Therefore, alongside the physical distinction between the performance space and reported space, we can also describe three *conceptual* spaces in tragedy: the private world of the *oikos*; the public world of the *polis*; and various kinds of outside world, usually less civilized than the world of the *oikos-polis*. A high proportion of the extant tragedies can be explained in terms of at least two of these three conceptual spaces: specifically, most of the plays to be set in a Greek city that were produced after the erection of the stage building.

This sense of conceptual space leads us to an interesting and, I think, important observation: when one of these plays reaches a violent climax, the violent act itself tends to occur *either* in private, inside the house, *or* beyond the walls of the city. I am aware of only one clear exception to this rule in extant tragedy: in Euripides *Suppliants* (which I discuss in the next chapter) Evadne throws herself to her death in the temple precincts – public spaces – of Eleusis. Another apparent exception is the on-stage suicide of Ajax in Sophocles' play of that name; but this event occurs following a scene change that takes us away from the public spaces of the Greek camp at Troy.[76] In *Oedipus the King*, the parricide took place years before at the place where three roads meet; Jocasta's suicide and Oedipus' self-blinding occur within. The public spaces of the city remain to this extent untouched by violence during the course of the action.

There is an obvious reason that tragic actions stay out of public space, and this has to do with staging: acts of spectacular and occasionally miraculous violence are more effectively described than enacted and therefore must take place off stage.[77] But this explanation will not entirely do, since the *eisodoi* do not only lead out of the city. Many reported events in tragedy take place (physically) off stage but still (conceptually) in public space; yet none of these events reported from public space are violent to the point of destruction. With the exception of Evadne in *Suppliants*, the nearest that violent acts in tragedy get to the public spaces of the city is at the very edge of these spaces. In two other plays by Euripides, *Phoenician Women* and *Trojan Women*, the young boys Menoeceus and Astyanax respectively jump and are thrown to their deaths from city walls. Some violent acts, it is true, are planned or discussed in public space. Usually the bodies are brought into the performance space – and therefore into public space – afterwards. But the city is spared these troubling events in themselves.

This structural sense of the security of the *polis* in tragedy illustrates a point that has been noted often before: the city is the perennial survivor in Greek tragedy; individuals and their households (frequently royal households) suffer, but cities survive.[78] There are exceptions, of course. Troy is referred to as a sacked city in many tragedies, but this is an Asian, not a Greek city. Only one Greek city is sacked (instead of merely attacked) in extant tragedy: Oechalia in Sophocles' *Women of Trachis*. The destruction of Troy, like that of Oechalia, is generally only referred to. Troy is destroyed as part of the very action of only one play: Euripides' *Trojan Women*, an extraordinary drama, which I discuss in the next chapter.

The place of the people in tragedy

The Greek word for the citizens of a *polis* is *dêmos*. A democracy (Greek *dêmokratia*, 'rule of the *dêmos*') was a city in which political power ultimately lay with an assembly that any citizen could attend; but oligarchies could have (less powerful) popular assemblies also (the Spartan assembly was known in the local dialect as the *damos*). When a Greek historian refers to a political decision made by a Greek city, he will normally say that, for example, 'the Spartans decided' or 'the Corinthians decreed'. The actions of a Greek army on the battlefield are generally attributed in the same way: 'the Spartans were victorious', 'the Corinthians encamped'. It was therefore quite usual to identify a city with its *dêmos*: the sum of its citizens. The politics of tragedy therefore should have something to do with the place of the *dêmos* in tragedy, and I consider this here. Of course, to represent several thousand people on stage carries its own dramatic problems. There are two ways, broadly, in which a poet could get around them: he could refer literally to the thoughts and actions of the people, located off stage; or a sense of the people could be communicated on stage in more indirect ways. I shall consider the latter category first.

One indirect means of representing the people is to exploit the sense of public space in the theatre. We have seen that the presence of the stage building creates a sense that everything that takes place in front of it takes place outside, in public. If a tragedy is set in a city and someone makes a public proclamation in this public space, then this proclamation can be felt to be heard by all the people, even if they are not in evidence on stage. This perhaps is what happens in the prologue of Aeschylus' *Seven Against Thebes*, where Eteocles addresses the people of the city. The chorus (in any case a chorus of women, not citizens) has not yet entered, and Eteocles appears to be addressing thin air. It is likely that in the first performance a small number of silent actors represented the citizens in this scene (they are sent to their posts at lines 30–5);[79] but a stronger sense of public space would have been provided by the theatre itself. Although *Seven Against Thebes* was produced probably before the erection of the stage building, which established an on-stage distinction between public and private space, the Theatre of Dionysus was a public space in a more literal sense: an outdoor, public area of Athens, inhabited during the festivals by audiences of citizens and others. There was no convention in Greek tragedy of direct address to the audience, so the audience cannot represent the *dêmos* in this scene. However, the general feeling of public space created by the presence of several thousand audience members is exploited here and elsewhere in tragedy.

It is often assumed that the people of a city are represented by the chorus of a Greek tragedy. However, the chorus members rarely, if ever, provide a literal representation of the *dêmos*. For one thing, twelve or fifteen chorus members cannot be expected to provide a close correspondence with thousands of citizens. For another, while it is true that a single actor addressing the chorus is an individual addressing a collective, this collective is always very closely defined. Any tragic chorus is homogeneous in gender, age and social status. More often than not, they are precluded from being representative of the citizen body by their status as women or slaves. Even in the extant tragedies that have male choruses, the men are usually elders of a city and therefore representative of the elite rather than the mass of citizens. This is the case in the two extant Aeschylean tragedies (*Persians* and *Agamemnon*) to have male choruses and in three of the five such plays by Sophocles.[80] The two military plays of Sophocles (*Ajax* and *Philoctetes*) provide exceptions to my rule, having sailor choruses, equal to the poorer Athenian citizens in the audience (see pages 92–3 below). One can add the chorus of Trojan guards in *Rhesus*, a tragedy attributed to Euripides but probably not by him. As for plays genuinely by Euripides, two have choruses that are elderly in age more than status: *Heracles* and *Children of Heracles* (compare page 49 above). All of the other surviving Euripidean tragedies have female choruses, with the exceptions of *Hippolytus*, where a male chorus appears only briefly, and *Alcestis*, which is not really a tragedy.

Although the chorus members therefore can rarely be equated with the *dêmos*, the chorus can sometimes represent the people in a less literal sense. Put briefly, they can speak for the citizens or be spoken to as citizens. At the end of the prologue of *Oedipus the King*, Oedipus summons the people of the city so that he can speak to them about the plague and the killer of Laius (line 144). Enter the chorus, who, although elders and therefore representative of the highest rung of Theban society, voice the hopes and fears of every member of the plague-ridden city (the *parodos*, 151–215). Oedipus then addresses them and issues the proclamation that he has called the people to hear (223 ff.). Sophocles thus exploits the public space of the performance area in the manner that I describe above; but he also allows the chorus members (plus any other, walk-on characters) to represent all the citizens for whom this proclamation is intended. Even non-citizen choruses can occasionally speak the thoughts of citizens. In Aeschylus' *Libation Bearers* the chorus of slave women celebrate not only the vengeance of Orestes but also the liberation of the people of Argos once the tyrants are dead (lines 863–5, 1046–7).

More literal means of representing the mass of citizens in tragedy must take the form of references to the people in reported space. This can occur easily in both military and political contexts. Just as the deeds of a citizen army in a reported battle can be attributed to 'the Thebans' or 'the Argives', the political decisions of democratic assemblies can be reported in the same way – as in Euripides' *Orestes* and in both of the plays (by Aeschylus and

Euripides) called *Suppliants*. In addition, we hear reports from military assemblies in plays such as Euripides' *Trojan Women* and *Hecabe*. (On Euripides' *Suppliants* and on *Trojan Women*, see the next chapter.) We can also hear reports of the people in a less formal sense. In Sophocles' *Antigone*, which has a chorus of loyal elders, the views of the people are not heard for a long time; they are finally expressed by the king's son Haemon, who breaks the news to his father that his actions have no popular support. The resonant voice of the people on this occasion has the effect of pricking the bubble of the king's rhetoric, previously associated with benevolence to the people. (On this and other aspects of *Antigone*, see again the next chapter.) This sense of a people with a resonant voice appears elsewhere in tragedy, in the context of both monarchy (Aeschylus, *Agamemnon* 938, compare 883–4) and democracy (Aeschylus, *Suppliants* 485): regardless of the constitution in each play, the politician is acutely aware of public opinion. In Euripides' *Orestes* the people even vote to execute the title character. One should add that this is a deeply ironic tragedy in all sorts of ways, and that Orestes has of course committed a terrible crime against his own mother; but he can also claim to be the next king of the city that condemns him. Oedipus never attracts the censure of citizens for his past actions in *Oedipus the King*, but he is still to some extent concerned about public opinion. He won the throne in the first place when he saved the Thebans from the Sphinx, a good deed to which he and others make reference (lines 35–6, 391–8). The people, through a priest who represents them in the prologue, expect him to save them again. Oedipus is anxious – at least earlier in the play, before his past overtakes him – to show himself a worthy king of his people.

Although the people of a tragic city can be a formidable body, it is interesting that they can rarely be held responsible for tragic suffering. For exceptions to this rule, we must look at late Euripidean tragedies such as *Orestes*, already discussed, and *Bacchae*, in which Dionysus holds the Thebans responsible for not worshipping him and sets in train the events that lead to Pentheus' gruesome death. Where cities are at fault in tragedy, I would argue that the blame lies more often in the person of a tyrant figure, who tends to be out of sympathy with his people: consider Sophocles' *Antigone*, which will be discussed in ch. 4. A more difficult example is provided by Euripides in *Heracles*, a play in which the people are factionalised by the tyranny of Lycus.[81]

These two brief discussions, of the city in dramatic space and the city as the *dêmos*, lead one to make two observations on the role of the *polis* in tragedy. Firstly, the city is a precious thing.[82] As we shall see in the discussion of *Antigone* in the next chapter, it could be conceived as the single source of a citizen's security and freedom. The safety of the city is frequently threatened – by war in many plays, by plague in *Oedipus the King*, by divine sanction in Euripides' *Bacchae* – but the Greek city always survives. Secondly, the people of the city are rarely at fault in themselves, but they can be a formidable body and an occasional source of insecurity to political leaders. Both city and citizens are treated in tragedy with a degree of respect.

A further problem: how can heroic drama be politically relevant?

Any attempt to locate the political in tragedy meets with one clear obstacle: the heroic setting. With the exception of Aeschylus' *Persians*, all the tragedies that survive are set in the world of myth, to which the political concerns of the fifth century ought to have been an irrelevance. The most obvious aspect of this irrelevance is the constitution of cities. Greek heroes other than Heracles tend to be actual or potential kings of cities; therefore heroic myths are set in monarchies. Fifth-century Greek cities, on the other hand, were for the most part either democracies or oligarchies (this included Sparta, whose two kings had military command more than political power). Monarchy in various forms survived only on the fringes of the Greek world, for instance in Sicily, Cyprus and Macedonia, the last of which was not really considered Greek at all.

The political starting point for any tragic poet was therefore monarchy, a more-or-less outdated form of government: this is the default political context of the plays. However, tragic poets could, if they wanted to, bring their drama politically closer to the present. The extent to which they do this varies from play to play and is almost always revealed in what might be called the internal logic of the drama. One means by which the political present can inform heroic drama is in the language used. For instance, Creon is first mentioned in Sophocles' *Antigone*, not as *basileus* or *tyrannos* or any of the other words for 'king', but as *stratêgos*. This was the fifth-century Athenian word for an elected general and so the official title of many contemporary politicians, notably Pericles.[83] Another means is not so much political as domestic. Most tragedies, we have seen, are set in somebody's household. These households, royal though they often are, tend to be of a type not wildly dissimilar to a fifth-century Athenian household: the father is at its head; the sons are expected to grow up to be like him; it is not always easy for women to come outside or speak to strange men;[84] they own slaves.

However, the most obvious way in which a tragic poet can bring heroic subject matter into the political present is by tinkering with the constitution of the city where the drama is set, tugging it away from the world of myth. Again, Aeschylus' Oresteian trilogy will serve as a useful case study. We have seen (in ch. 2) that the idea of justice at the start of the trilogy is broadly the same as the one held by heroes in the Homeric epics, which were composed well before the classical period, and that this idea is updated by the end of the trilogy to resemble the judicial model favoured in democratic Athens. The constitution that provides a political home for this justice changes accordingly. At the start of the first play Agamemnon is still the king of Argos. When he returns the chorus address him as king. They also reveal a tension between the respect that is due to a conqueror and the risk of heroic excess (782–9):

> Behold, my king: sacker of Troy's citadel,
> Own issue of Atreus.
> How shall I hail you? How give honour
> Not crossing too high nor yet bending short
> Of this time's graces?
> For many among men are they who set high
> The show of honour, yet break justice.

The possible excesses of kingship are thus condemned in the language of *dikê* (justice), the major theme of the trilogy.

However, Agamemnon will soon be killed and replaced as ruler by Aegisthus and Clytemnestra. The entrance of Aegisthus, attended by an armed bodyguard and addressing threats to the chorus members, will have put a fifth-century audience in mind of the tyrants that ruled many Greek cities in the seventh and sixth centuries BC. One might compare a twenty-first century play that made frequent and obvious reference to the twentieth-century political phenomenon of fascism: the audience would immediately understand the political and cultural references (compare the discussion of Don Taylor's TV production of *Antigone* in ch. 5). To a mid-fifth-century Greek theatre audience, tyranny was the shared political experience of their parents and grandparents. In *Libation Bearers*, the second play, the chorus celebrates the end of tyranny at Argos (as we saw on page 81).

The third play, *Eumenides*, provides a more specific and contemporary political environment. Following a prologue set in Delphi, the scene shifts to an Athens that bears close constitutional resemblance to the democratic city. In particular, the role that Athene plans for the Areopagus council as a homicide court is identical with that council's only important function following the reforms of Ephialtes only a few years before the trilogy was first staged (see ch. 2). The trilogy thus moves through several hundred years of Greek history, from kingship to tyranny to democracy.

Although in the internal logic of a play the dramatist can dictate terms with reasonable freedom, we can also get immediate clues from the setting. Of the Greek tragedies that are set in cities, a very high proportion is set in Argos, in Thebes or in and around Athens. The original audience would have had expectations of the way these cities were run. For instance, tyrannies in tragedy, other than Argos under Aegisthus, tend to be Theban. Democracies tend to be Athenian but can almost as easily be Argive.[85] However, the internal logic of a play can develop in ways that jar with expectations and alter the audience's idea of what kind of a city this is. Here are two examples.

The default political context of heroic drama, we have seen, is monarchy. In Aeschylus' *Suppliants* (which I introduced in the last chapter) Pelasgus introduces himself as 'ruler of this land' (line 251) and goes on to describe the extent of his kingdom. He thus appears to place Argos in this default context. However, the government of this city is more complicated than that. When the chorus of suppliants asks that he does not give them up to the sons of Aegyptus (thus risking war), Pelasgus refuses to do so without first consulting the people. The chorus' reply is made still under the assumption that he is able to wield absolute power (365–75):

KING: It is not *my* house at whose hearth you sit; and if
 The Argive State stands liable to guilt herein,
 The people of Argos must together work its cure.
 Therefore I'll undertake no pledge till I have shared
 This issue in full council with my citizens.
CHORUS: *You* are the state, *you* are the people.
 Ruler unquestioned, you control
 The altar that is your country's hearth;
 You fear no vote; by your mere nod
 You, monarch on one throne, decide all issues
 Therefore, guard against guilt.

But Pelasgus is wary of leading his people into war without their consent (398–401):

KING: I have said already, though I am sole king, I cannot
 Act in your case without my people. May my citizens
 Never, if some mischance befell us, say to me,
 'You destroyed Argos for the sake of foreigners.'

Only when the chorus persuade him of his obligation towards suppliants (and threaten to hang themselves if he does not honour this obligation) does Pelasgus act. And even here his action is to address the assembly just as a democratic politician would. Pelasgus may not be constitutionally bound to consult the people, but he still feels a strong compulsion to do so.[86] Certainly the political context of the play cannot be guessed at before the action begins and is only gradually made apparent.

Sophocles' *Oedipus at Colonus* is set in the place that gives its name to the drama, which happens to be Sophocles' home village. This is a patriotic play and we might expect to witness democratic government as we do in Euripides' *Suppliants*, a tragedy which is also set in Athenian territory. The question is settled in the prologue, just after Oedipus has been told where he is (lines 66–7):

OEDIPUS: Have they a sovereign, or does the word rest with the people?
STRANGER: They are ruled by the city's king.

Here, the concept of democracy is not unknown to Oedipus, for all that he was brought up in the royal court of Corinth and is the mythical former king of Thebes; but the possibility that this Athens is a democracy is closed off within the first hundred lines of the drama. Whereas democratic assemblies made decisions on the advice of public speakers, the local men who form the chorus of this play quickly defer to their king, Theseus (lines 294–5). When the man appears, the executive nature of his power is confirmed by the speed and decisiveness of his actions.[87]

One form of constitution that never appears in tragedy is oligarchy. This is perhaps surprising, since in various forms it was the most usual way of running a Greek city in the fifth century. Part of the reason has to do with the Athenian context of the original performance. Until the short-lived oligarchic revolution of 411 BC, oligarchy did not really feature on the Athenian ideological radar: they acknowledged tyranny as the polar opposite of democracy (a solemn curse was pronounced against tyranny at every meeting of the Athenian assembly). After 411, the law against setting up a tyranny was changed to one of subverting the democracy.[88] Even in *Oedipus at Colonus*, written and produced after 411, Oedipus (see above) can only conceive of monarchy and democracy as possible forms of government. Thus in Euripides' *Suppliants*, where Theseus, 'king' of an Athens that otherwise seems quite democratic, debates the merits of democracy with a Theban herald, the position that the herald adopts is not pro-oligarchy but pro-monarchy. Classical Thebes was essentially an oligarchy and had escaped the tyranny that affected many Greek cities before the fifth century. Why then is the city misrepresented? I shall look at this question in the next chapter, and consider ways in which oligarchy possibly does feature; but a major reason must be that, to Athenians in the audience, monarchy presented a more satisfying contrast with democracy.

The natural political home of tragedy was therefore heroic monarchy. It was possible, however, to manoeuvre the drama into forms of tyranny or democracy. In those few tragedies that are set in a clearly democratic city, it seems that more of a direct appeal is being made to the majority Athenian component in an international audience. It follows that, where tragedy slipped back into the world of heroic monarchy, more universal political questions could be raised.

CHAPTER 4

FOUR POLITICAL TRAGEDIES

Introduction

We can now look at some tragedies in depth, taking a political perspective. We must bear in mind our working definition of 'the political' as 'a concern with human beings as part of the community of the *polis*'. This definition, however, is only our best fit: we must not be too disappointed if a clearly political play appears to transgress it. I have chosen four plays, two by Sophocles and two by Euripides, that yield a variety of political readings. Some of them have been mentioned already in the previous two chapters. In each case, there are three questions that we can ask immediately; the answers may provide important clues to the politics of the play. First, when was this play first performed? Second, broadly, what is the political environment of the play? And third, what is the political identity of the chorus members? I will also outline the plot of each play before discussing its merits as political drama in more detail.

The observations I will make across the four dramas may occasionally differ from or even contradict each other; for, if it is in the nature of drama to present several points of view at the same time, it is also likely to provoke them. If I am right, then the didactic function of tragedy goes no further than to make the audience think: a view closer to the Euripides than the Aeschylus of Aristophanes'

Frogs (see ch. 1). This should still allow us to identify some political issues of interest to the tragic audience. Discussion of these four tragedies will therefore increase our understanding of Greek popular political thought, as well as of the political in tragedy.

Sophocles, *Ajax*

Although we do not know when *Ajax* was first performed, it is generally acknowledged to be one of the earlier Sophoclean plays that survive. It dates perhaps from the 440s BC, when Sophocles had already been producing plays in Athens for around twenty years.[89]

The answer to the second question (on the political environment) is interesting and not so brief. The drama appears immediately to fail to fit our working definition of 'the political': although the play is concerned with human beings as part of a community, this community is not a *polis* but the Greek military camp during the Trojan War. But the military camp could in fact be considered as a kind of *polis* at war. Consider the following two points: in the Greek imagination the city was the sum of its male citizens; and the military was representative of large parts of the citizen body, everyone except the old and the infirm. We can go further: the army was not just representative of citizens, but (as we saw in the last chapter) it *was* notionally the city in military guise. A military tragedy therefore has a political dimension. One should observe additionally that the Greek camp at Troy is comprised of representatives from many Greek *poleis*, not just one. The focus of the drama, however, is on the affairs of the Salaminian contingent; it is onto this scene that other Greeks intrude.

One aspect of the political that would normally be missing from the military camp is the domestic. (I argued in the last chapter that the *oikos* was a building block of the *polis* and that most political dramas are simultaneously domestic.) In fact a kind of surrogate family features strongly in this play, so that a typically tragic polit- ical outlook is preserved. Ajax has a replacement wife, Tecmessa, a prisoner of war who lives with him in the camp. Such spear- won brides would not have seemed strange to the ancient Greeks, especially in the context of the Greek camp at Troy: Homer's *Iliad* begins with a quarrel over just such a woman. Here the role of the wife is extended to meet the conventions we are used to from other tragedies. She has a young son by Ajax, Eurysaces, who does not speak but nevertheless performs several important dramatic func- tions (principally in an early scene with his father, lines 530–95, and later when Teucer instructs him to supplicate Ajax, now dead, lines 1168–84). The first half of the play is set in front of Ajax's tent: hence we have a surrogate house to go with the surrogate house- hold. The stage geography of this play thus mimics the setting of more obviously political dramas, as described in the last chapter.[90] We might therefore refer to the Greek camp in this play (and the Salaminian contingent within it) as a 'political community'.

As for the third question, the chorus are Ajax's men; in fifth- century terms they are citizens at war. Further, they are described as sailors as well as soldiers, which seems surprising: the Greek forces have arrived at Troy by sea but most of their exploits take place on land.[91] However, the choice of a sailor chorus might have jarred less with an Athenian audience for the following reasons. First, we can note that these sailors come from the island of Salamis, which by the fifth century was part of the Athenian city-state. Ajax was one of the ten heroes after whom the ten tribes of Athens were named in the democratic era. In one of the choral odes (starting at line 596), the men sing in honour of this island; in another, they express a wish to return to Athens (1216–22).

Second, the strength of Athens was in its navy as well as its army. The military backbone of the typical Greek city was its hoplites, or heavily armed soldiers. These men tended to be at least moderately wealthy, for they needed to maintain their own armour and weapons. In many Greek cities the military role of poorer citizens was reduced to carrying light arms; this kept them out of the hand-to-hand fighting that was the main feature of hoplite warfare. Athens, on the other hand, had kept a very large fleet since the mid-480s and used this fleet to maintain a sea empire (see in ch. 1 above). Oarsmen were needed for this fleet, and the thetes (roughly the poorer half of the citizen population) were the natural sailor class. These citizens (together with men from allied cities who also rowed) were therefore at least as important to the city as its hoplite army. Although Athens had been a democracy for some twenty years before the expansion of its navy, the military role of the thetes should not be underestimated when one considers the strength and durability of popular rule in the years that followed. In other words, it was hard for a Greek city to be ruled only by the rich if its power and prosperity relied on the service and potential sacrifice of poor men.[92]

Ajax is a play about a hero who, feeling insulted when the arms of the dead Achilles are awarded not to him but to the lesser hero Odysseus, tries to take violent revenge on the army that made this decision by ballot. Fortunately for the army, the goddess Athene drives Ajax temporarily mad and he succeeds in rounding up and killing some cattle and their herdsmen. The loss of honour is so great that Ajax kills himself. A striking feature of *Ajax* is that the action begins when this story is already well underway, when Ajax has finished his killing spree but has not yet come out of his madness; so the drama deals not with the madness itself but with its aftermath. One can contrast two Euripidean tragedies, *Heracles* and *Bacchae*, in which a character is deluded by a god and kills unwittingly. In both of these plays the madness and the killing come comparatively late, followed by a final scene in which the killer comes to terms with what he or she has done. *Ajax* might similarly have finished with the suicide or soon after, but at that point the play seems to stop and start all over again with a new plot line: the question of his burial. This restart is preceded by a scene change and by the exit and re-entry of the chorus; it is further emphasised by the entry of a new character, Ajax's half-brother Teucer. He presses the case for burial in the face of opposition first from Menelaus and then from Agamemnon. These brothers, known collectively as the Atreidae (the sons of Atreus) are joint commanders of the Greek forces. They are thoroughly opposed to burying a man who tried to do such a dreadful thing to them.

The long debate over the burial also allows Sophocles to reintroduce a character who appeared in the prologue: Odysseus, the winner of the ballot over the arms of Achilles. He favours the burial and uses his influence to see that it goes ahead. This comes as an almost complete surprise, since Odysseus was Ajax's greatest enemy among the Greeks. It also plays against expectations of the untrustworthy character usually associated with Odysseus in tragedy. Sophocles has already introduced us to an enlightened Odysseus in the prologue, where he pointedly refuses to laugh at Ajax's misfortune. In the final scene of the play Odysseus is more reasonable still. He gives three reasons for supporting the burial of an enemy: that Ajax was a great hero, that not to bury the hero is irreligious (compare Antigone in Sophocles' play, discussed below) and that a similar fate could easily come to him (see lines 1316–73).

What brings unity to this play in two parts? The thrust of the plot is towards the rehabilitation of a fallen hero.[93] Ajax's honour is at its lowest ebb as the play begins. Suicide, as far as he is concerned, is the way out of this predicament; but his reputation is only restored when, as the play closes, his burial is secured. It is interesting for the present purpose that the obstacles placed in the way of his burial are political obstacles. Menelaus and Agamemnon appear not just as powerful men but also as the speakers of essentially political arguments. These arguments are discredited in various ways, not least by the unsympathetic nature of the speakers.[94] The Atreidae, however, do not accept contradiction and only back down on the advice of Odysseus.

Menelaus' speech forms the first part of an exchange of views with Teucer. He forbids the burial of Ajax on the grounds that he turned against his comrades and, but for divine intervention, would have killed them all (1053 ff.). Ajax could not be controlled when he was alive, says Menelaus, but at least he can be ruled when dead (lines 1067–70). The speech continues (1071–86):

> And yet it is the mark of someone bad
> That, common though he is, he will not think
> It right to listen up to those who are
> In charge. For never, neither in the *polis*
> Could laws be held up well, except where fear's
> Established there; nor could an army be
> Commanded any longer with good sense,
> Except when held by awe and reverence.
> And here's another thing: a man should think
> That – mighty though he is in body – he
> Could stumble even from a slight misfortune.
> Fear, that's the thing, and also shame. The man
> Who cleaves to these is safe, you see? But when
> He breaks the bounds and does whatever thing
> He wants, then see how soon our *polis* here,
> Which sails before fair winds, will take a fall
> Into the depths. Still, may a timely fear
> Exist in me as well. And let's not think
> That doing what we like we won't again
> Know suffering and punishment and pain.

In some ways these lines make a lot of political sense. Although it is surprising that Menelaus refers to the military camp specifically as a *polis*, we have seen that the description is appropriate. His central observation, that collective security comes with collective discipline, would have seemed sensible enough to the member of a Greek city-state: see further the discussion of Sophocles' *Antigone* below. The introduction of fear as a source of order in the city would not have offended a Greek, even in democratic Athens. The Greek word used repeatedly here for fear is *deos*, which has connotations of reverence as well as alarm. This word appears in the same context in one of our central sources on democratic ideology, the Periclean funeral speech (Thucydides 2.37, in the translation of Rex Warner; he renders the word as 'respect'):

> We are free and tolerant in our private lives; but in public affairs we keep to the law. This is because it commands our deep respect (*deos*). We give our obedience to those whom we put in positions of authority, and we obey the laws themselves, especially those which are for the protection of the oppressed, and those unwritten laws which it is an acknowledged shame to break.

This idea appears also in another key democratic text: Aeschylus' *Eumenides* (lines 696–703, quoted on page 62, and compare lines 517–28). Here Athene, like Menelaus in *Ajax*, associates a healthy fear closely with safety for the city. As in Pericles' funeral speech, the fear Athene has in mind is a kind of respect both for the law and for persons in authority (in Athene's case this means the Areopagus council[95]).

Although Menelaus' speech has similarities with these democratic texts, his language sounds distinctly undemocratic, especially in the way he sets himself up as an authority figure above the common man. To describe a hero like Ajax as 'common' (*dêmotes*,

line 1072) is in any case bizarrely inappropriate. Menelaus' equa-
tion of the camp and the *polis* appears more than anything to suit
his own rhetorical purpose. Teucer in his reply makes the obvious
point that Ajax is king of his own people and, although obligated to
the Atreidae by oath, cannot be bossed around by them (1097 ff.).
Menelaus' pompous tone and over-confidence in his own authority
find an echo in (again) Sophocles' *Antigone* with the character of
Creon; and are put into perspective by the admission that he is only
able to behave towards Ajax in this way now he is dead (contrast
Odysseus at 1347, whose stance has softened since Ajax died).[96]

Agamemnon, in the next scene, begins with an attack on Teucer's
credentials: how can he, whose mother was a slave, question the
authority of Menelaus (1226 ff.)? This argument in itself has a
bearing on questions of status and citizenship, as we saw in ch. 3.
Agamemnon's next point builds on the argument made by Menelaus
(1239–49):

> To our demise, it seems, did we announce
> A competition for Achilles' arms
> Among the Greeks, if we on Teucer's say
> Are everywhere considered bad and you,
> Defeated though you are, will never wish
> To yield in front of this majority
> Decision of the judges. I suppose
> That you will either keep abusing us
> Or wounding us with your deceit, although
> You lost. Of course, from practices like these
> There is no way in which the institution
> Of any law could come about – if we
> Reject the rightful winners and bring forward
> The losers from the rear up to the front.

The simple point is that Teucer is a bad loser and should respect the decision of the judges. (Teucer does call the conduct of the vote into question at line 1135, although this accusation is never substantiated in the play.) It is tempting to cast this as a democratic decision, since the judges voted,[97] but I think a broader point is being made about respect for established authority and the law: these principles are put at risk, argues Agamemnon, if we are to concede to Teucer. Agamemnon, like Menelaus, seems at first sight to argue reasonably, although his words should be considered in the light of the abusive language that precedes them.

Thus, in two successive scenes, potentially reasonable arguments on the necessity of respect for political authority are discredited by the context in which they are given and the characters of the speakers.[98] This should not lead us to conclude that behind *Ajax* is an anti-political message, a rejection of authority and law. (After all, for everyone to behave as Ajax does would be a recipe for anarchy.) The hero himself may be fiercely individual, but in many other ways *Ajax* is a play about how to live with other people: in a political community this, on my definition, becomes a political issue. *Ajax*, as well as being great drama, is a text on Greek citizenship. The agenda is set in the *parodos* (157–61, quoted already in ch. 2):

> Envy stalks
> After magnates of wealth and power;
> Yet humble men without their princes
> Are a frail prop for a fortress. They
> Should be dependent on the great,
> And the great should be upheld by lesser ones.

The idea of the interdependence of great and lesser men anticipates Ajax's dependence, after his death, on Teucer and Odysseus to secure his burial. It also suggests the chorus members' views on how their own society works. Following the hero's suicide their own sense of dependence on Ajax echoes that of Tecmessa, who worries for her son, Eurysaces, and fears enslavement to the Atreidae (944–51):

TECMESSA: Poor little one! What a yoke of servitude
  We go to! What hard taskmasters!
CHORUS: They are ruthless indeed, the two sons of Atreus,
  If they do the unspeakable thing
  You have spoken in your distress:
  God forbid!
TECMESSA: Even in what we suffer I see the gods' hand.
CHORUS: Yes, they have given an overload of grief.

Ajax is aware of the imperative for interdependence, as he shows us in the so-called 'deception speech' (646–92, see pages 52–3 above), which in turn is a response to the persuasive claims on his familial loyalty made by Tecmessa at 485–524. By committing suicide, he actively resigns his responsibilities to his family and to his men.

A very different example is set by Odysseus. Some modern scholars have described the characters of Ajax and Odysseus respectively as competitor and co-operator.[99] Ajax's competitive instinct seems to come directly from the Homeric idea of heroism: every hero strives to be the best there is and, crucially, to win gifts as material representations of his peers' recognition of his greatness. Ajax is without question a greater hero than Odysseus; therefore in heroic terms he receives an unbearable insult when the Greeks fail to award him the arms of the only one of his contemporaries to be greater still. Odysseus, on the other hand, shows an ability to compromise and thus seems better equipped for life in the community of the fifth-century *polis*. The difference between heroic and classical society can be conceived in terms of aristocracy on the one hand and political community on the other; that is to say, only in the former is it necessary that the top man stands head and shoulders above the rest.

This contrast has been explained plausibly in terms of the nature of fifth-century warfare.[100] In Homer the heroes are all kings of individual Greek cities and lead their people into battle, but they appear to fight as individuals. The great exploit of the Homeric hero is the *aristeia*, a period of action in which one hero single-handedly influences the course of the fighting. Homer's mythical account perhaps reflects the realities of an earlier Greek society, in which the rich and powerful had the greatest leisure to train for battle and greater resources with which to equip themselves. The Homeric hero even has a chariot in which to arrive at the fighting and, having fought on foot, make a quick getaway.[101] In archaic and classical Greece, by contrast, the rise of a wealthy middle class was reflected in the development of hoplite warfare.[102] The hoplite phalanx depended for its success on two things: numbers and co-operation. Each hoplite went into battle equipped with heavy armour, a sword and spear, and a large round shield held in his left hand. Whereas Homer represents his heroes as men who fight for themselves and their own glory, the hoplite moved as part of a unit and fought, quite literally, for the men on either side of him. The shield covered not only part of his own body but also that of the man to his immediate left. In a vivid illustration of the principle of co-operation, a hoplite depended for survival on the man to his right, just as the man to his left depended on him.

But would Ajax as competitor have been such a fish out of water in the fifth-century *polis*? The classical Greek cities did not suppress the heroic instinct to compete so much as regulate and exploit it: witness for example the popularity of the Olympic games and other inter-city sporting contests.[103] Democratic Athens in particular made a great success of harnessing the competitive nature of its elite citizens and using it for the greater good of the city. An example comes from the very festivals at which the tragedies were performed. It will be remembered, importantly, that the tragedies were presented in competition with each other. We saw in chh. 1 and 2 that the chorus for each tragic poet at the Dionysia or the Lenaia was paid for through the *leitourgia* of a wealthy individual called a *chorêgos*. This man shouldered some of the great expense of presenting a tetralogy of plays and won considerable prestige for himself if the tetralogy won. Another important type of *leitourgia* was the financing of warships: while the muscle behind the navy came from the poorer citizens, the timber and sails came from the very richest.

A very different means of regulating the competitive instinct of the elite was provided by the institution of ostracism (temporary exile, on which see ch. 1). It is important not to see ostracism as a punishment – an ostracised politician had done nothing wrong, nor was he unpopular: like the loser in a modern election, one *could* say he was the second most popular politician of the day. Ostracism was invented and practiced for various individual political purposes; it did not happen every year and after 443 BC (around or just after the probable first performance of *Ajax*) only one ostracism was held. However, its very existence as an institution suggests that the Athenians were aware of the damaging effects of political competition, as well as the benefits.

We see then how the competitor / co-operator dichotomy relates to the values of the fifth-century *polis*. How clearly did this come across to the audience on the day? It is difficult to say. If we accept the view given in Aristophanes' *Frogs*, the political function of tragedy is to teach its audience how to be good citizens; more specifically, characters that appear on stage provide examples of citizen behaviour. As I noted in ch. 3, it is hard to see how tragic heroes like Ajax can come across as model citizens. For one thing, Ajax is so great – physically and heroically – that no normal person could hope to emulate him; for another, his actions in the play go disastrously off the scale in terms of anti-social behaviour. Thus both the quali-

ties for which we can admire Ajax and the actions for which he must
be condemned make him a difficult example of citizenship. The kind
of reading proposed by Mark Griffith (see ch. 2) offers a way around
this problem: ordinary audience members would have sympathised
with Ajax but would not have tried to emulate him; instead they
would have taken the point of view of the chorus members, loyal
sailors whose fortunes are closely linked to those of their leader. We
have seen how the Athenian thetic class might have identified with
the chorus of this play; but in a democracy some citizens, at least,
were as likely to see themselves as equal with the political players
– Agamemnon, Menelaus and Odysseus – as they were to subordi-
nate themselves and their own security to a more heroic figure.[104]
Odysseus' ability to compromise seems purpose-built for city living
and he certainly presents a more realistic example of citizenship
than Ajax. My best guess is that, on the one hand, Ajax – like any
tragedy – was designed to provoke the Aristotelian emotions of pity
and fear in its audience, and therefore to facilitate collective experience. The political response, on the other hand, would have been as
varied as the membership of the audience.

Ajax is a difficult play to read politically. It is set in the camp of
an allied army: exactly where political authority lies here is unclear,
a point of debate between Menelaus and Teucer. The play brings
together a peculiar mix of heroic and political values: the simplest
expression of this is that Ajax is like a competitive Homeric hero
who is transported uncomfortably into the world of the fifth-
century polis (or its military equivalent), in which he is ill-equipped
to survive.[105] But, if anything, competition was encouraged in
the polis; in addition, the self-styled champions of civic order,
Agamemnon and Menelaus, are just as motivated by a heroic desire
to compete and win. Even Odysseus' actions are associated in the
play with his aristocratic status: noble in both senses of the English
word.[106] Perhaps the most difficult point of interpretation of Ajax

as a political tragedy is that apparently sensible arguments for the rule of law are received so unsympathetically, while the audience's sympathy is directed to a clearly antisocial individual. We can remind ourselves that the dramatist is not expected to present his ideas as logically as the writer of pure political theory.

The play can certainly be read as an exploration of citizenship, specifically the interdependence of the members of a political community. A starting assumption of this exploration seems to be that some men are more powerful than others: not a very democratic sentiment, but one that reflected the reality of any Greek city-state. A possible conclusion (I would not go so far as to call it a 'message') is that loyalty within the family or neighbourhood might lead us to question conventional political authority. It is interesting that this conclusion should be reached in a play by Sophocles: of the three canonical tragedians, he was the only one to hold high political office himself (as a treasurer of Athene in 443/2, as a general two years later and as one of the special legislative panel – the *probouloi* – appointed in 412). To explore these issues further we can turn to another play by Sophocles: *Antigone*.

Sophocles, *Antigone*

The traditional date of the first performance of *Antigone* is 442 BC. This date is given on shaky grounds, however: a biographer from later antiquity claims that Sophocles was elected general following the success of the play. We do have reliable evidence that Sophocles served as general in 441/0. The story that he became general as a result of *Antigone*'s success remains hard to believe, but it becomes at least plausible – plausible enough for a later scholar to include it in his biography of Sophocles – if *Antigone* was indeed first performed in 442 (but not 441, when first prize went to Euripides).[107] This also fits with most attempts to date the play based on the evolution of Sophocles' dramatic style. This was an important moment in Athenian history. The year before had seen the ostracism of a prominent politician called Thucydides son of Melesias (the patronymic is generally given to distinguish him from the now better-known Thucydides, the historian). This removed the last obstacle to the unchallenged influence of Pericles among the Athenians. This influence would extend for more than a decade, almost until his death in 429; although neither Sophocles nor his audience can have known this in 442, we can with caution find some relevance to Periclean politics in *Antigone*.

The play is set in the aftermath of conflict between the sons of Oedipus. This battle is a popular subject in tragedy. It is foreshadowed in Sophocles' *Oedipus at Colonus* and described in various different ways in Aeschylus' *Seven Against Thebes* and Euripides' *Phoenician Women*, as well as the first chorus of *Antigone*. Following the death of Oedipus, his sons Eteocles and Polyneices agreed to rule Thebes in turn, each for a year at a time. When the first year ended, and Polyneices returned, Eteocles refused to yield the throne. Polyneices returned to his adoptive home of Argos, raised an army and marched on Thebes. In *Antigone*, the brothers have both died in the battle. The new ruler is Creon, brother-in-law of Oedipus (see the family tree in Appendix C).

Questions of the political environment and the political identity of the chorus can be answered with reference to the beginning of Creon's first speech (162–74):

> Gentlemen: as for our city's fortune,
> The gods have shaken her, when the great waves broke,
> But the gods have brought her through again to safety.
> For yourselves, I chose you out of all and summoned you
> To come to me, partly because I knew you
> As always loyal to the throne – at first,

When Laius was king, and then again
When Oedipus saved our city and then again
When he died and you remained with steadfast truth
To their descendants,
Until they met their double fate upon one day,
Striking and stricken, defiled each by a brother's murder.
Now here I am, holding all authority
And the throne, on virtue of kinship with the dead.

This Thebes is a monarchy, as it usually is in tragedy. Further, there
is general acceptance in this play that the king speaks for the city.
In the prologue, opposition to his decree (on which, see below) is
taken by his niece Ismene to be the same thing as opposition to the
power of the citizens (line 79):

To act in defiance of the citizenry;
My nature does not give me means for that.

She perhaps means the same thing at line 44, where she says
that the burial of Polyneices is 'forbidden to the city' (the Greek
could just as easily mean 'forbidden *by* the city'). But can this king
claim such a level of authority? Creon has recently become king,
as he puts it, through 'kinship with the dead': he is a relation by
marriage to the previous kings, Laius, Oedipus and Eteocles. His
sister's marriage certainly provides him with a property claim on
the throne in the absence of a direct male heir (the language he uses
would have put an Athenian audience in mind of their own law of
inheritance[108]), but there was no direct succession. The vagueness
surrounding his constitutional status is reflected in the way he is
addressed and described by Ismene's sister Antigone. While other
characters describe him as a king and address him as *anax* ('my
lord', 'sir'), Antigone first describes him as a *stratêgos* (general) and
otherwise refers to him as 'Creon'.[109]

The chorus members are elders of Thebes, summoned as we see here by the new king because of their track record of loyalty to previous rulers. Although their loyalty to Creon is stretched during the action, they remain essentially his people. They might be expected to act as Creon's advisers, but they have no influence on his government until quite late in the action.

Creon has a very simple policy in the aftermath of the battle. The first and last principle by which Creon rules Thebes is the safety of the city (182–91; one can compare Menelaus in *Ajax*):

> And anyone thinking
> Another man more a friend than his own country,
> I rate him nowhere. For my part, God is my witness,
> Who sees all, always, I would not be silent
> If I saw ruin, not safety, on the way
> Towards my fellow citizens. I would not count
> Any enemy of my country as a friend –
> Because of what I know, that she it is
> Which gives us our security. If she sails upright
> And we sail on her, friends will be ours for the making.
> In the light of rules like these, I will make her greater still.

Consequently, Creon's first act as king is to provide burial with full military honours for Eteocles, who died defending his city, and to decree that nobody shall bury Polyneices, who led a foreign army against his own people: his body will be left outside the city walls to be eaten by birds and wild animals. Of the heroes' two sisters, Ismene wishes to do what she is told but Antigone resolves to bury her brother. She does this as well as she can. When some guards expose the body once more, she returns to the scene and this time is caught in the act. Creon sentences her to death. She will be sealed in a remote cave with only minimal food and drink, but not before she has defended her actions in the following terms (446–57):

CREON: Now, Antigone, tell me shortly and to the point,
    Did you know the proclamation against your action?
ANTIGONE: I knew it; of course I did. For it was public.
CREON: And did you dare to disobey that law?
ANTIGONE: Yes, it was not Zeus that made the proclamation;
    Nor did Justice, which lives with those below, enact
    Such laws as that, for mankind. I did not believe
    Your proclamation had such power to enable
    one who will someday die to override
    God's ordinances, unwritten and secure.
    They are not of today and yesterday;
    they live forever; none knows when first they were.

To a modern audience, Antigone comes across as a plucky individual who stands up for what is right before an autocratic ruler. This view, however, is informed by a peculiarly modern, western idea of the relationship between the individual and the state: this is to assume that the state has no business meddling with our (harmless) personal freedoms; we associate such oppression with fascist or communist dictatorship. In particular, the powerful and public ideology of one western country, the United States of America, was developed in this spirit (even before the advent of fascism and communism). To the ancient Greek, on the other hand, much of Creon's speech above would have made perfect sense. The speech in fact could be quoted with approval by the fourth-century orator Demosthenes (*On the False Embassy* 247). At the heart of Creon's argument is the point that 'our country *is* our safety'. The USA, in common with some other modern states, was founded on the principle that human beings have inalienable rights; the primary purpose of its constitution and therefore its laws is (this is the ideal) to protect these rights. The ancient Greek notion of rights, such as it was, did not tend towards the universal and inalienable. To them, the only real guarantor of an individual's freedom was the laws of the city in which he happened to live.[110] If he was a citizen of that city, he was free; if he was a foreigner or if the city was ruled by a tyrant, he was less free. In Athens, for instance, a metic had to register with a citizen as a kind of legal sponsor and pay an annual tax to the city.

If the city was the only guarantor of individual safety and freedom, then one's first duty was to the city. Behind Creon's simple 'city first' message is a more sophisticated point: if one looks after the city, then the city will certainly look after the individual and one's family; but if one puts oneself or one's family first, one could possibly endanger the city. The historian Thucydides attributes a similar point to Pericles (Thucydides 2.60):

> My own opinion is that when the state is on the right course it is a better thing for each separate individual than when private interests are satisfied but the state as a whole is going down hill. However well off a man may be in his private life, he will still be involved in the general ruin if his country is destroyed. On the other hand, so long as the state itself is secure, individuals have a much greater chance of recovering from their personal misfortunes.

It should be stressed that the speech from which these words are supposed to come (not the funeral speech but a second Periclean speech from book 2) was made in the year 430, more than a decade after what we assume to be the first performance of *Antigone*; further, this is only Thucydides' version of what Pericles is meant to have said. Nevertheless, 'city first' is a plausible and popular ideology for a politician of the time to have embraced, as we can see from Sophocles' play.[111] The difference in *Antigone* is that awkward questions are asked of this ideology.

Awkward questions come in the first place from Antigone herself.

In the famous 'unwritten laws' speech, part of which I have quoted on page 107, she suggests that, notwithstanding the view I outline above, there are universal duties (if not quite rights) that must be observed: the city is not necessarily the first and last arbiter of what is right for its citizens. Quite what Antigone means by 'unwritten laws' is not entirely clear and perhaps does not matter. The phrase appears to have been popular among contemporary speechmakers and had the great advantage that one could use it to refer to anything or nothing at all.[112] For example, the Thucydidean Pericles uses a similar phrase in part of the funeral speech (Thucydides 2.37, quoted above on page 96), but that should not be taken to mean that Pericles is deliberately echoing Antigone or means the same thing as she does. What does matter to Antigone is that to leave a body unburied offends some universal and unshakeable principle, authored by the gods.

A second, equally damaging question must be asked of the 'city first' ideal when we consider the leadership style of Creon, which seems hostile to the very subjects he is supposed to protect. Creon is a fearsome ruler, which perhaps explains the chorus' failure to advise until late in the play. Creon finishes his opening speech by forbidding the burial of Polyneices. The chorus replies (211–4):

> Son of Menoeceus, so it is your pleasure
> To deal with foe and friend of this our city.
> To use any legal means lies in your power,
> Both about the dead and those of us who live.

These men are noted for their loyalty, but even they stop short of praising Creon's words. Their reply can be paraphrased colloquially as, 'Whatever you say, Creon, you're the boss'. Antigone will later claim that only fear of their king prevents them from disagreeing openly (line 509). Another demonstration of the effect of Creon's manner on his subjects comes from one of the guards who first discover that Polyneices' body has been buried. The guards draw lots over who should report the matter, so uneager are they to face Creon. The unlucky loser appears on stage in timorous mode, saying that he several times had to persuade himself not to go back on his errand (223 ff.). Creon cleverly, if unreasonably, holds the guard responsible until such time as he can produce a culprit; he only releases the guard from guilt when Antigone, now on stage, admits her crime (444–5).

A still more damaging blow is to come. After Antigone has been condemned, but before she goes to her death, we meet Creon's son Haemon. Haemon is betrothed to Antigone and clearly in love with her. The news that Haemon brings is crippling to Creon's only recently established sense of authority: the people, unanimously it seems, support Antigone's stance and find Creon's decree unreasonable (693–70). Haemon is the only person brave enough to break this news; he implies that the people are too fearful to make their views known themselves (690–1). Creon hardly notices when Haemon tells him that the people support Antigone, mistaking Haemon's words for pure youthful insubordination. When Haemon repeats the point, Creon reacts more angrily (732–9):

CREON: Is *she* not tainted by the disease of wickedness?
HAEMON: The entire people of Thebes says no to that.
CREON: Should the city tell me how I am to rule them?
HAEMON: Do you see what a young man's words these are of
   yours?
CREON: Must I rule the land by someone else's judgement
   Rather than my own?
HAEMON: There is no city
   Possessed by one man only.
CREON: Is not the city thought to be the ruler's?
HAEMON: You would be a fine dictator of a desert.

Creon's mistake was to assume that, since he is on the side of the city, the city in turn supports him.[113] Haemon's revelation entirely undermines Creon's assumption. He falls back on the view that his authority is synonymous with the authority of the city ('Should the city tell me how I am to rule them?'). This reasonable view, we have seen, is shared by Ismene in the prologue at line 79. But Creon goes further: he claims that the city should be ruled in its king's interests, it belongs to him. Creon has moved from a reasonable point of view, that the city must come first, to the claim that the city exists to serve him. How did he reach this position? We have already begun to see how inconsistent and unfounded his position apparently is. This leads us to two further points.

First, it may be that Creon always ruled Thebes for himself, despite the rhetoric.[114] In the first part of his first speech (which I quote above, pages 104–5) we get a sense, not just of a policy of putting the city first, but also of Creon's autocratic implementation of this policy. Line 173 of the Greek ('Now here I am, holding all authority / And the throne') betrays his view of what monarchy is: absolute power.[115] If Creon has given nobody else even the smallest stake in the rule of Thebes, one wonders if he always saw the city as his personal domain; this goes further than Ismene's implicit identification of the word of the monarch with the power of the citizens.

Second, Creon was mistaken in the first place: not only do the citizens fail to support him, but he was never really on the side of the city at all. It is easy for us as the audience to make a similar mistake. A bold misreading of the play constructs a conflict between *oikos* and *polis*, with Antigone and Creon the respective champions of these institutions.[116] Creon's actions, however, do not help the city so much as threaten it. In the scene that comes after Haemon angrily leaves the stage, we see Antigone give her last speeches before going to her death. Then comes a new figure: the blind prophet Teiresias. He warns of a danger to the city resulting from

Creon's policy: birds have taken carrion from Polyneices' corpse and deposited it on the altars in the city, so that the gods will no longer accept Theban sacrifices. And perhaps we did not even need Teiresias to tell us that Creon's policy might be bad for the city. A possible lesson learnt from Sophocles' *Ajax* is that one can promote cohesion among citizens by agreeing to the burial of one's enemies; Creon rejects this opportunity. Creon's policy might not have seemed so wrong to Athenians in the audience, who had a law against burying traitors on Attic soil.[117] But there were ways in which one could be flexible: Creon could for instance have allowed Polyneices' body to be buried outside Theban territory.

Nor does Antigone threaten the city. To bury Polyneices is accepted as right by all the citizens (according to Haemon) and even by Creon later in the play. Her disobedience certainly does pose a threat to the authority of the man in charge – but is this the same thing as a threat to the city? We have seen that Antigone's language casts doubt on Creon's status as a king. It also casts doubt on Creon's instruction not to bury Polyneices, which she almost always refers to not as a *nomos* (law) but – more accurately – as a *kerugma* (proclamation, decree). An exception is in the 'unwritten laws' speech, at line 452, where she deliberately echoes Creon's 'this law' in order to draw a contrast with divine law. Antigone's opposition, therefore, is not to the laws of the city but to one man's decree. We have seen by contrast that Ismene (at line 79) associates Creon's power with that of the citizens. Antigone later appears to use her sister's very words, acknowledging that she buried Polyneices in defiance of the 'power of the citizens' (*bia politôn*, line 907); these words, however, come in a passage taken by many editors not to be the original work of Sophocles. Even if the passage is genuine, Antigone is less well informed than Haemon, who has been among these citizens (line 692 – as a man he will have spent far more time in public life than the two sisters).

Difficulties accumulate for Creon and his civic policy, but that is not to discredit 'city first' as a political principle. The problem is not

so much in the principle itself as in Creon's misguided interpretation of it and his intransigent pursuit of this interpretation. If it is
in the nature of tragedy to present agonisingly extreme situations,
it can also test the most reasonable ideas to extremes: we saw this
in *Ajax* and now we see it in *Antigone*. Thus Sophocles can ask difficult questions of popular political morality without undermining
it entirely. Just as Ajax's actions confirm, not deny, the need for
cooperation between the powerful and the less powerful, so we can
detect the city's very real need for protection behind Creon's flawed
leadership of it.

Nor is it easy entirely to blame Creon, since the audience's
sympathy rests with him long (in dramatic terms) after Antigone's
tragic death. Creon at first responds angrily to Teiresias but later
sees sense and, following his elders' advice probably for the first
time, rushes to bury Polyneices and rescue Antigone. He reaches
the cave too late. Antigone has hanged herself, it seems, without
waiting to starve to death. Haemon is found there, crazed and
grief-stricken. Creon begs him to leave the cave. There now comes
one of the most dramatic deaths reported in tragedy: Haemon does
not reply, but first spits in his father's face, then lashes inconse-
quentially with his sword and finally turns his sword on himself.
This news reaches home and, in reaction, Creon's wife Eurydice kills
herself too. Creon is left alive to lament his dead family and what
he now recognises as his own folly.

Antigone seems at first sight to have no special relevance to a
democratic audience. Creon does not resemble a democratic politician: decisions are made by him alone, without the involvement of
the people. At the one point of collective decision-making, it is a
case of a small circle of elders advising him, not of him advising the
whole city. We can only find relevance to the Athenian democracy in
the Thebes of this play if we consider Creon as a tyrant. Any Greek
of the fifth century would have approved seeing a tyrant meet his

ruin, but perhaps a democrat more than most would appreciate the competing assumptions, made by Ismene and Haemon, of popular support and opposition.

Several modern scholars have considered Creon to be a tyrant.[118] This view certainly seems tenable on both of the definitions I give in ch. 1. He does not directly inherit the rule of Thebes but, like many sixth-century Greek tyrants, takes over following an aristocratic power struggle. His autocratic style of rule can also be taken as tyrannical. In addition, Creon is anxious from the outset to show that he is on the side of the city. This again is most clearly reminiscent of a seventh- or sixth-century tyrant, who, in the absence of a strong claim on the throne, needed to justify his rule as an act of benevolence towards the city. However, one important aspect of tyranny is missing: the bodyguard. A tyrant's bodyguard is a mark of his insecurity; Creon on the other hand is fatally over-secure in his trust in popular support.

A final political resonance is more specific, and has to do with the way in which Creon formulates his 'city first' policy. The similarities between Creon's first speech and Thucydides 2.60 are not, I would suggest, entirely coincidental. There is no direct Periclean influence on Sophocles – Pericles gave his speech years after the probable first performance date of *Antigone* – but the Thucydidean speech can be taken as an indication of a fashionable political principle of the time. This principle can be stated as follows: the city is one's principal source of safety; one therefore ought to do what is best for the city; only if the city is safe can we ourselves and our households be safe. I hope to have shown how Sophocles picks holes in such assertions, without entirely discrediting them.

Euripides, *Suppliants*

Like *Antigone* (and unlike Aeschylus' *Suppliants*) Euripides' *Suppliants* deals with the aftermath of the battle between Eteocles and Polyneices. In *Antigone* the burial of Polyneices is at stake; in *Suppliants* we are concerned with the safe return and burial of seven men, for Polyneices was one of seven heroes to attack Thebes. The chorus, after whom the play is named, are the mothers of the dead heroes. Their interests are pressed by the man who led the expedition: Adrastus, king of Argos and father of Polyneices' widow. Argos has been weakened so much by the war that Adrastus turns to Athens and King Theseus for help. As a result, and as we shall see, the play takes on a special relevance to Athenian politics.

Theseus is hard to persuade. He questions Adrastus and finds out that the attack on Thebes by the seven was made in the face of unfavourable sacrificial omens (lines 155–9). In the end, women move him to pity where a man has failed. Having listened to the suppliant women and persuaded by his own mother, whose name is Aethra, Theseus commits his city wholeheartedly to the retrieval of the heroes' dead bodies. This pattern, of reluctance followed by deliberation followed by resolution, could be portrayed as an Athenian virtue,[119] as we see from part of the Periclean funeral oration (Thucydides 2.40):

> We Athenians, in our persons, take our decisions on policy or submit them to proper discussions: for we do not think that there is an incompatibility between words and deeds; the worst thing is to rush into action before the consequences have been properly debated.

Piety is also displayed as an Athenian virtue. Theseus' initial condemnation of the attack on Thebes (lines 229–31) is couched in terms of Adrastus' defiance of the gods, his neglect of unfavourable omens. Theseus responds at the end of the play to Athene – who appears as *dea ex machina* – in pious, obedient terms (1227–31). In addition, the imperative to bury the dead, whatever they have done wrong, is repeatedly – as in Sophocles' *Antigone* – associated with divine law (for example, at lines 16–19). However, the play differs from *Antigone* in its emphasis on human law. We have seen that in *Antigone* Creon's instruction on the burial of Polyneices takes the form of a decree, not a law. The essential opposition in *Antigone* is therefore not between god's law and man's law, but between god's law and the decree of one man. Euripides' *Suppliants*, by contrast, presents us repeatedly with an idea of a human law held by all of the Greeks, or even by all men. This idea is closely associated with a notion of divine law close to that held by Antigone. (We must assume that – like Antigone's imperative to bury dead brothers – it is an unwritten law, for there was no authority for the codifying of international law in ancient Greece.) For example, when Aethra persuades her son to accept the suppliants, she argues in terms both of honouring the gods ('for if you slight them you will fall', lines 301–2) and of 'what all Greece holds lawful' (311). Theseus, in his long speech to the Theban herald, talks of upholding 'the law of all the Greeks' (526–7, words repeated by an Athenian herald to the Theban army at 671–2). He finishes the speech with an appeal to 'that ancient law / Established by the gods' (561–3). Thus god's law and man's law are in agreement in this play.

An important aspect of Theseus' decision to help the suppliants is his promise that the Athenians will risk their lives in battle, if need be, to complete this mission. We saw in ch. 2 that, as part of the Athenian self-image, the city was especially willing to harbour suppliants and to back this policy up with force. Theseus is reluctant to use force until more peaceful means have been exhausted. First comes an inconclusive encounter with a Theban herald (mentioned already in ch. 3 and discussed below). Unable to succeed by diplo-

matic means, Theseus leads the Athenians against Thebes. The
Athenians win the battle and bring back the bodies for cremation.
The play reaches a tragic climax when Evadne, one of the widows of
the seven, throws herself on her dead husband's pyre. At the end of
the play Adrastus is instructed by the goddess Athene to swear an
everlasting alliance between Athens and Argos.

I shall answer my three questions this time in reverse order.
Instead of a chorus of men, either sailors or elders, the chorus here
are the suppliant women. This, however, is no less political a drama.
The chorus of this play has a far more dynamic dramatic role than a
chorus of elders might have: they may not advise the king, but they
do supplicate him. We may never see the male citizens of Athens,
but we do hear about their political and military exploits, so that the
citizen body features strongly in the drama. Theseus is an undoubtedly political figure, on any definition of that term.

The political environment of the play is as democratic as is found
in tragedy. Theseus may nominally be king of Athens but he has
given power to the citizens. This is what he says when he decides
to help the suppliants, even if it takes the city into war (lines
349–53):

> I desire the city
> With all its voices to approve this plan.
> It will approve because I want it to:
> But if I state my reasons, I shall have
> More favour from the people, whom I made
> Sole rulers when I set them free
> And gave them equal votes.

This is an extraordinary speech, and not just because we learn that
Theseus has given his kingdom to the people (this is not the only
account of Theseus as the mythical founder of democracy[120]). One is
struck most of all by his supreme confidence that they will follow his

proposed course of action, even if it means committing them to war
with Thebes. Unlike Pelasgus in Aeschylus' *Suppliants*, who needs
to persuade his own people (see ch. 3), Theseus knows beforehand
that he can win this approval simply because of who he is; he does
not even need to state his case. This presents a tension between
the supposed rule of the masses and the unassailable influence of
one man. This difficulty might plausibly be explained in terms of
Thucydides' appraisal of Pericles' rule (Thucydides 2.65): that 'in
what was nominally a democracy, power was really in the hands of
the first citizen'. In opposition to this view, it has been pointed out
that Pericles had been dead for nearly a decade by the time *Suppliants*
was produced and that Thucydides' appraisal was not yet known by
the Athenians;[121] but I think the connection can still be made. By
the 420s BC, the Athenians must have become used (if Thucydides is
even half right) to following the advice of one great politician; even
if that man was now dead, it was now easy to see how a single great
leader could become an important democratic figure. That is not to
say that the Euripidean Theseus in any way represents Pericles; only
that the legacy of Pericles helps us to make sense of him.

And this tension makes historical sense in other ways. Under
the real democracy, the character and reputation of an orator must
have made a big difference.[122] In other words, the assembly would
take advice as much because of public confidence in the adviser as
the quality of his argument, although of course these two factors
were closely linked (consider Cleon in 425, whom I discuss at the
end of this section). Further, most orators came from the social
elite, at least until the rise of the 'new' politicians, of whom Cleon
was one;[123] in other words, at least some of the advice given to the
people came from the very sort of men who would have ruled them
under an aristocracy. Similarly, the most influential orator in the
Athens of Euripides' play is the king. He has given up the power of
monarchy but retained its influence.

The play was first performed at some point in the late 420s BC, and probably before peace was made with Sparta and her allies (including Thebes) in 421. This rather uncertain date is potentially more crucial than it at first appears to be. We cannot, and need not, date the play precisely enough to link it to any specific historical event; but we can place a particular development in Athenian political thought broadly in the mid-to-late fifth century. It was around this time that questions concerning the best form of government for a city began to be formalised in writing. It is hard to say exactly when this development took place, since we do not have access to everything that was written and some of the surviving works cannot be dated accurately. In addition, any intellectual development is bound to have taken place in spoken discourse, perhaps for some time, before being recorded in writing; so the rise of literary constitutional theory may reflect more broadly a rise in informal constitutional debate. This is turn was part of an ongoing intellectual revolution in Athens at the time.[124] Undeniably, the question was not merely theoretical; the debate could be forced by events, even before the oligarchic revolution in Athens that occurred in 411 (around a decade after *Suppliants* was first performed). For centuries before, the two archaic Greek phenomena of tyranny and colonisation must in their different ways have exercised Greek minds on constitutional questions. The very introduction of democracy and, perhaps more tellingly, the international success of democratic Athens gave a particular shape to these questions. Hence the historian Herodotus could write as follows, commenting on an early military success for democratic Athens (Herodotus 5.78):

> Thus Athens went from strength to strength, and proved, if proof were needed, how noble a thing equality before the law is, not in one respect only, but in all; for while they were oppressed under tyrants, they had no better success in war than any of

their neighbours, yet, once the yoke was flung off, they proved the finest fighters in the world.

So the Athenian interest in constitutional theory may have gone back as far as the beginnings of democracy in 507 BC.[125] The literature of the late fifth century, however, appears to reflect an increasing interest in, and formalisation of, this question.

Two prose works of the time provide evidence that a debate on constitutional theory was becoming formalised. Both authors show an ability to argue for or against the merits of at least one type of constitution. Neither can be dated with great precision but they are both roughly contemporary with *Suppliants*, the one somewhat earlier, the other maybe a little later. The earlier contribution is again from Herodotus, an exact contemporary of Euripides who lived for some time in Athens. He died no later than 415 BC and may have left Athens for good as early as 443 in order to join the new colony of Thurii (here he may himself have helped to write the constitution). However, it is likely that Herodotus had read parts of his work to Athenian audiences by the 420s. In book 3 of his *Histories*, following a coup d'état in Persia, the seven leaders of this revolution discuss what form of constitution Persia should now have (Herodotus 3.80–2). Three of them make proposals: one for democracy, one for oligarchy and a third (the future King Darius) for monarchy. Each sets out the advantages of his proposed system and points out the disadvantages of the others. Herodotus protests (in such a way that we can almost hear the dissenters at an early recitation) that this conversation really did take place; that seems unlikely, if only because the nature of the debate is far more redolent of Greek fifth-century political discourse than anything that would have been said in Persia in the sixth century. However, whatever the shortcomings of this episode as history, it is highly instructive as one of the earliest writings in European political theory.

The second prose work is called *The Constitution of the Athenians* and is found in the writings of Xenophon, but is most probably not by him. The author (familiar already from ch. 2 of this book) is universally known to modern scholarship as the 'Old Oligarch' – although the one thing that we can say about him with reasonable certainty is that he was a young man. The work is notoriously difficult to date; most attempts place it somewhere between the 440s and 415 BC.[126] It seems clear that the author was an Athenian, or at least a resident of Athens (he occasionally refers to the Athenians as 'we'), writing for an actual or implied audience of non-Athenians. While denouncing democracy as a bad form of government that puts power in the hands of the undeserving poor, he is able grudgingly to acknowledge the success of the Athenian system.

These two pieces of prose – the latter a mere pamphlet, the former just a small part of a sprawling work of history – anticipate the full-scale works of political theory that would be written by Plato and Aristotle in the fourth century. It seems inevitable that, as a highly political medium, tragedy should also have contributed to the debate at least once.

The appearance in *Suppliants* of the herald from Thebes begins a debate, which from his first words is framed in terms of rule-by-one and rule-by-all (lines 399–408):

HERALD: What man is master in this land? To whom
　　Must I give the words I bring from Creon, ruler
　　In Cadmus' country since Eteocles
　　Fell at his brother Polyneices' hand
　　Beside the seven-mouthed gates?
THESEUS:　　　　　　　　　　One moment, stranger.
　　Your start was wrong, seeking a master here.
　　This city is free, and ruled by no one man.

The people reign, in annual succession.
They do not yield the power to the rich;
The poor man has an equal share in it.

The translation here (by Frank William Jones, in the Chicago University Press series) uses 'master' for the Greek *tyrannos*. Going by the definition I give in ch. 1, a *tyrannos* (tyrant) was a sole ruler who did not inherit his position. However, poets used the word with less precision than this, and in tragedy it tends to be used in an ideologically neutral sense for 'king'. 'Tyrant' might therefore be too strong a word to translate *tyrannos* in this passage. If so, there is no clear signal here that the herald speaks for tyranny, the 'bad' form of monarchy (on which see ch. 1). On the other hand, the opposition of democracy with rule-by-one (an anachronism in mainland Greece by the fifth-century) would immediately have put the audience in mind of tyranny, which democracy replaced at Athens. It is likely that this dramatic debate was understood by the original audience as one between democracy and tyranny.

Following the opening remarks, the exchange between Theseus and the Theban herald takes the form of an *agon*. An *agon* (the word means 'contest') is a debate in a tragedy or comedy following certain formal rules. In a tragic *agon*, two opposing speeches of equal length are given, each followed by a short remark from the chorus. The debate usually descends into more rapid exchanges, with the result that each party tends to leave the scene more angry and more entrenched in his or her position than before. Sophocles sometimes makes use of an *agon* (for instance, between Menelaus and Teucer in *Ajax*, or Haemon and Creon in *Antigone*) but it is a form of which Euripides appears to have been especially fond. The possibilities for political drama unlocked by this form are, of course, immense. If Euripides applies an *agon* to constitutional debate only once in sixteen or seventeen surviving tragedies, this only reflects the range of suitable topics, some more political in substance than others, that arise from plot developments.

The debate is between a political system where the people have a master and one where the people *are* the master. Thus the constitution of Athens is brought up to the present day, while Thebes suffers under apparent tyranny; this contrasts with the real Thebes in the fifth century, which had an oligarchic government. The explanation I gave for this in the last chapter (pages 88–9) was that public expressions of the political ideology of Athens before 411 took tyranny to be the polar opposite of democracy and did not acknowledge oligarchy in the same way. To misrepresent Thebes as a tyranny made even more sense in the years when Athens was at war with Sparta and other oligarchic cities, among them Thebes: the tyrant was a more effective political bogeyman than the oligarch.

To squeeze three into two in this way is necessitated not only by the prevailing ideology but also by the dramatic form of the *agon*: it cannot contain the kind of three-sided debate conducted by the Persian nobles in Herodotus. Given a choice between a democracy-oligarchy *agon* and a democracy-monarchy version, it is natural to choose the latter, which presents a starker contrast. But does oligarchy still creep into the debate? It might be that the one dichotomy is superimposed on the other.[127] Consider again these lines from Theseus' first speech to the Theban herald (405–8):

> This city is free, and ruled by no one man.
> The people reign, in annual succession.
> They do not yield the power to the rich;
> The poor man has an equal share in it.

The first line here establishes that Athens is no monarchy. The second is a clear reference to the Athenian style of democracy, in which public officials as well as the 500 members of the council were chosen annually by lot. The third and fourth lines, however, seem to refer to oligarchy. In a Greek oligarchy, membership of the ruling elite was typically based on a property qualification. An oligarchy was therefore the rule of the rich; a democracy was the rule of the rich and poor, but could be characterised (especially by its detractors) as the rule of the poor.[128]

So Theseus appears to elide tyranny with oligarchy. He does this in another way at the beginning of his *agon* speech (lines 429–37). Here he says that monarchy is all very well in a primitive society, where one man alone dispenses justice, but the introduction of written laws gives rise to equality before the law. Theseus further insists that where there are laws the case is won by the citizen with the right argument, not the citizen who is rich. Theseus thus claims the rule of law for democracy. In fact, the same claim could be made for oligarchy (see for instance Herodotus 7.104 on the Spartans). Theseus' implicit point seems to be that the rule of law under oligarchy is less developed than it is under democracy, which provides actual *equality* of law.

This suggests a second way in which Euripides might be squeezing a three-sided debate into a two-sided *agon*. Both democracy and oligarchy could be presented by Greeks as defences against tyranny, which therefore stood conceptually apart form the other two forms of government. Oligarchy goes unmentioned in this play – as elsewhere in tragedy – but an implicit contrast is perhaps made: by promoting the claims of democracy as an opponent of tyranny, Theseus leaves one to suppose that oligarchy is a second-best means of promoting political freedom.

Theseus goes on to celebrate one of the cornerstones of Athenian democratic ideology (438–9):

> This is the call of freedom:
> 'What man has good advice to give the city,
> And wishes to make it known?'

This is a tragic formulation of the question given by a herald at the beginning of any meeting of the Athenian assembly: 'who wishes to speak?' (*tis agoreuein bouletai*?) – the point being that anyone could. To the democratic ideology of *isonomia* (equality under the law), we can then add *isêgoria* (equality of speech). Neither of these exact words appear in Theseus' Greek but the concepts come across clearly. Both of these words were sometimes used as synonyms for *dêmokratia*.[129]

Theseus makes three other points. Democracy provides no threat to able young men; the tyrant, by contrast, might want to dispose of them as potential rivals. Democracy provides no threat to personal wealth (viewed with envy and suspicion by tyrants) or to the integrity of the family (a danger commonly associated with tyranny[130]). These three points taken together reinforce an impression of Athenian ideology that is a little closer to the idea of a modern liberal democracy than is sometimes acknowledged by many (including me perhaps, elsewhere in this volume). There were indeed limits on personal ambition and personal wealth in Athens, but these only affected the super-influential and rather unlucky (through ostracism) or the super-rich (through the obligation to provide a *leitourgia*).

Before the start of the formal *agon*, the herald points out some disadvantages of democracy: democracy allows self-serving politicians to win favour with the people through flattery (lines 412–17); the people themselves are incapable of political judgement (418–22); therefore only worthless men attempt to pander to them (423–5). There are interesting comparisons to be made (here very briefly) with Aristophanes' comedy *Knights* (see ch. 2), which was produced in 424, around the same time as *Suppliants*. It is unclear whether Aristophanes approved of democracy or not, but he is certainly able to point out some structural weaknesses in a radical democracy led by influential orators.[131] The Theban herald's first point (on unscrupulous flattery) is the premise of the whole of *Knights*; but his second point (on the political ignorance of the people) is ultimately dismissed by Aristophanes (see for example the choral ode at *Knights* 1111–50).

Much of the herald's case in the *agon* proper rests not on the merits of monarchy but on the advantages of avoiding conflict. He does, however, make one point about the democratic mechanism for declaring war (476–85):

> Think now: do not let anger at my words
> Goad you to puffed-up answers. You are free;
> That does not make you powerful. Hope has driven
> Many cities against each other; she stirs
> An overreaching heart; she is not to be trusted.
> When the people vote on war, nobody reckons
> On his own death; it is too soon; he thinks
> Some other man will meet that wretched fate.
> But if death faced him when he cast his vote,
> Hellas would never perish from battle-madness.

The Theban herald's argument here is weak. In a fifth-century context, to doubt that Athens could be a powerful city seems absurd, at least (as we are about to see) before 415. The terms of the herald's statement (freedom does not necessarily engender power) also directly contradicts Herodotus in the passage (5.78) quoted above. More to the point, it could be presented as one of the *strengths* of democracy that the very people who might be risking their lives in battle chose whether or not to declare war.[132] This perhaps is what is meant when the Thucydidean Pericles talks about debate and action (Thucydides 2.40, quoted at the beginning of this section).

However, it is possible that a more subtle point is being made about the Athenian decision-making process. This can be illustrated with reference to an episode that took place a few years after the first production of *Suppliants*. In 415 the Athenians decided with some enthusiasm to launch an ambitious expedition that then would add the whole of Sicily to the empire. The assembly heard speeches for and against the venture (the debate is described at Thucydides 6.8–26) and voted to launch a massive fleet, unaware that this fleet would be destroyed at Syracuse two years later. Euripides could not have foreseen this disastrous episode when he was writing *Suppliants*; but this event does serve to indicate how easily the Athenians could be persuaded to adopt ambitious war plans. Another example comes from the time when *Suppliants* was first produced. The Athenians were soon (in 421) to make peace with Sparta. They were in a strong position to do this, since they had been holding 120 Spartan hostages since the Battle of Pylos in 425. That the peace took so long to come can to a great extent be explained in terms of Cleon's proposal to ram home the advantage further and the Athenians' enthusiastic reception of this proposal. Cleon's ability to win this argument rested in turn on his own prestige as the victor at Pylos.[133]

Aside from constitutional affairs, the politics of Euripides' *Suppliants* works on a further level: citizenship. We have already seen that Sophocles' *Ajax* offers various models of citizen interaction. *Suppliants* provides more specific detail. Here, for example, is a description of the responses of different citizens to the question of whether to go to war. In this passage Theseus, speaking to Adrastus about the attack on Thebes, shows himself to be as concerned about bad decision-making as the herald is (232–45):

> You were led astray by glory-loving youngsters,
> Promoters of unjust wars, who spoil the townsmen.
> One of them wants to be a general;
> Another to seize power and riot in it;
> A third is set on gain. They never think

What harm this brings for the majority.
The classes of citizens are three. The rich
Are useless, always lusting after more.
Those who have not, and live in want, are a menace,
Ridden with envy and fooled by demagogues;
Their malice stings the owners. Of the three,
The middle part saves cities: it guards the order
A community establishes.

This is one of several places where Adrastus is described as having been led astray by the belligerent energy of young men: a lesson, perhaps, for the Athenians. The preoccupation with self-serving politicians seems similarly close to the views of the Theban herald, except that Theseus shows greater concern for the safety of the majority. To idealise a middle class between the elite and the impoverished might seem less what we would expect from a democrat; but this is a typically Greek expression of a 'golden mean' between two extremes (compare Euripides, *Heracles* 588–92, where the characteristic vices of the very richest and the very poorest are associated with support for tyranny). Of more interest perhaps is the *role* Theseus ascribes to this broad middle class: to preserve the established order. The implication is that the rules by which a city is governed should be followed faithfully, regardless of the constitution of that city; Theseus for a moment speaks to a broader agenda than the democratic.

The desirability of a golden mean between wealth and poverty informs much of the longest discussion of good citizenship in the play. This is where the bodies of the heroes have been brought back and Adrastus remembers the virtues that each man had. His description here adopts a more moderate tone than the picture of youthful impetuosity we had before: even the warlike Tydeus is described euphemistically as 'wise in deeds, not words' (line

908). Elsewhere we get some sense of the variety of types of good citizen, desirable in any Greek city (860–80, these lines speak for themselves):

The handsome one is Capaneus. Through him
The lightning went. A man of means, he never
Flaunted his wealth but kept an attitude
No prouder than a poor man's. He avoided
People who live beyond their needs and load
Their tables to excess. He used to say
That good does not consist in belly-food,
And satisfaction comes from moderation.
He was true in friendship to present and absent friends;
Not many men are so. His character
Was never false; his ways were courteous;
His word, in house or city, was his bond.
Second I name Eteoclus. He practiced
Another kind of virtue. Lacking means,
This youth held many offices in Argos.
Often his friends would make him gifts of gold,
But he never took them into his house. He wanted
No slavish way of life, haltered by money.
He kept his hate for sinners, not the city;
A town is not to blame if a bad pilot
Makes men speak ill of it.

Euripides' *Suppliants* is unusual among the tragedies that survive for the depth of its engagement with constitutional theory. It also goes further than any of the others in presenting Athens as a democracy. But it also shares many political themes with other plays. Athens in this play is not only a democracy but, as elsewhere in tragedy, a resolute supporter of those that supplicate her. Theseus, Athens' legendary king, is a pious and sound leader, as in other plays: Sophocles' *Oedipus at Colonus* or Euripides' *Heracles*. (The exception is perhaps Euripides' *Hippolytus*, a less political play, set away from Athens.) *Suppliants* also looks beyond Athens, placing a strong emphasis on panhellenic law (and Athens as its enforcer). Lessons – applicable across the Greek world – are learnt concerning the effects of good citizenship and good counsel on the fortunes of a city. Thus qualities of piety and good judgement are attributed to some of the dead heroes as well as to Theseus. These men are remembered as citizens as well as soldiers.

Euripides, *Trojan Women*

Trojan Women takes as its theme the fate of the wives and daughters of Trojan heroes after the sack of Troy. It is an extraordinary tragedy. Seemingly very little happens: only the killing of Hector's young son Astyanax is a complete action in the sense that the decision, the deed and the reaction take place during the course of the play. The decision of the Greeks in assembly is reported at lines 709 ff.: Odysseus urged them not to allow their enemy's son to live (the implication is that a grown-up Astyanax could take revenge on them). Astyanax is hurled from the ruined walls of Troy, and at line 1118 the body is brought on stage. A Greek herald (Talthybius) and the Trojan women arrange a hasty burial. Otherwise the dialogue concentrates on remembering what is past, learning what has already happened and finding out what is yet to happen. Of what has already happened, Queen Hecabe hears that her daughter Polyxena has been killed on Achilles' tomb as an offering to the dead hero. As for events to come, the women are told with which Greek heroes they are each to be enslaved. Another future event is revealed in the prologue through a dialogue between the gods Athene and Poseidon. During the war, Athene had taken the Greek side, Poseidon the Trojan side. But in the destruction of

Troy the Greek hero Ajax, son of Oileus (not to be confused with the better-known Ajax, son of Telamon, the subject of Sophocles' play) dragged the Trojan princess Cassandra forcibly away from Athene's temple and raped her. The Greeks failed to punish Ajax, and so Athene asks Poseidon to send a storm to wreck the Greek fleet. This seemingly rather static play therefore has a sense of purpose in several respects. It would have made all the more dramatic sense at the first performance, where *Trojan Women* was the conclusion of a connected trilogy around the theme of the Trojan War.

As most of what we find out in the play has either already happened or is yet to happen, it is appropriate that the action fills a very definite timeframe: just as the Greek ships are loaded with booty and slaves to take home from Troy. The precise sense of time is underlined by the lack of the usual tragic cityscape: Troy is a ruin and the Greek camp that does form a backdrop will cease to exist at the end of the play.[134] The action ends as the last of the Trojan women join their ships and the destruction by fire of that great city is completed. The victory of the Greeks appears to be comprehensive; the audience is left to remember for themselves what the gods have in store for them.

The political environment of any play set during the Trojan War is a special one. As in *Ajax*, the Greek heroes are all kings of their own cities but are fighting in an alliance under the leadership of Agamemnon. As for the Trojans, Priam, now dead, was the enormously rich and powerful king of that city. Both these political contexts, however, are suspended at the time of the play: the Greek alliance is breaking up in order to go home; and Troy is as extinct as its dead king.

The chorus members are the Trojan women of the title, along with four named characters: Hecabe, Cassandra, Andromache and Helen; only Helen is slightly different, as she was born Greek and will be taken back by her original husband, Menelaus. Following the prologue, the action is based around three episodes and the *exodos* (final scene). The three episodes feature respectively Cassandra, Andromache and Helen. Hecabe, Priam's widow, remains on stage throughout as interlocutor. Until Menelaus appears, two-thirds of the way through the action, we see only one man, the herald Talthybius. He represents the unseen Greek heroes and conveys their dreadful decisions, but he is hardly a hero himself (heralds by convention did not fight). In fact, in his reluctance to break bad news, Talthybius emerges as a surprisingly sympathetic character.[135] When Menelaus enters, it is a jarring intrusion into a female scene, an impression reinforced by his occasionally crass and disrespectful comments. The extent to which the action takes place amongst women is further underlined through reference to absent men: Hecabe's late husband Priam, Andromache's Hector and Helen's Paris.[136]

So this is an unambiguously female drama. How can it be political? It might help to consider the date of the play. *Trojan Women* was produced in the spring of 415 BC, when Athens was nearing the end of an uneasy period of peace with Sparta. During the preceding winter the Athenians had added the Aegean island of Melos to their empire. Melos was originally founded by the Spartans, and the Melians had tried to remain neutral during the war. When they refused to be taken over without a fight, the Athenians responded brutally, killing all the men they captured and enslaving the women and children. It is this grim detail that finds an obvious correspondence with Euripides' play.

Can we be sure that this correspondence is deliberate? There is no reference or even allusion to Melos, even though Euripides shows himself able to make contemporary references in this play. There is a perhaps rather gratuitous mention of Athens, contrasted favourably with Sparta (lines 208–13); and of Sicily, a possible allusion to the expedition that was soon to leave for that island (220–3).[137]

Furthermore, there are few points of comparison between Troy and Melos: the former was a magnificent Asian power, against which a coalition of Greek cities fought a lengthy war over the claims on his wife of one man; the latter was a small Greek island, easily subjected by one city in a display of imperial prowess. In fact it is easy for modern readers to overestimate the importance of Melos to the Athenians at the time. This event is well known mainly through the importance Thucydides gives it in his *Histories* and especially because of the famous 'Melian Dialogue' (Thucydides 5.84–113), a dramatised reconstruction of the discussions between the Athenians and the Melians, which precedes his brief record of the Athenian blockade of the island. In turn, the Melian dialogue allows Thucydides to illustrate the aggressive imperialism of the Athenians. However, Euripides' audience was not yet familiar with Thucydides' history, so we must put it from our minds.

On the other hand, it is hard to see how the play at its original performance could not have put some members of the audience in mind of recent events at Melos: many of them would have been in the assembly when the relevant decisions were taken and many others would have been on service with the fleet. It is also possible that a number of the enslaved Melian women and children were working in Athens by that time, either as public slaves or in private houses.[138] If Euripides *did* have Melos in mind, he could hardly have made this clear in the course of this tragedy without insulting the Athenian people, who were ultimately responsible for what had happened. (As we saw in ch. 2, the Athenians do not appear to have enjoyed being criticised in front of other Greeks.) We must conclude that it is impossible to know Euripides' intentions in writing the play; however, we can ask easier questions concerning the possible impact of the drama on its original audience.

Like *Antigone*, *Trojan Women* has an obvious modern resonance, which would not quite have made sense to a Greek audience. The play has been performed frequently in the modern era at such times and in such a way as to provide commentary on the conduct of modern wars (see ch. 5). Something similar may have been meant by its first performance, but in two respects the values behind the commentary are not the same.

The first point is that the modern political doctrine of pacifism would have meant little to most ancient Greeks. Warfare was almost a fact of life in the ancient world; many or most Greek men would take part in armed conflict during the course of their lives, an experience that the vast majority of people living in the modern West have never had. In Homer's *Iliad* the heroes can complain about the misery of war but also celebrate the glorious military deeds of themselves and others; the two views were quite compatible.[139] (Similar views are expressed by Cassandra in *Trojan Women*, lines 365 ff.) So, while Greeks could certainly find war brutal and even futile, they were unlikely to argue that it was in itself immoral. Nor were the Greeks likely to distinguish between a just and an unjust war. Ancient morality was no respecter of national boundaries: the question was not whether one should invade other people's territory but whether one could do so with impunity. To conquer could be damaging to the national pride of the conquered; but empire-building was not generally resented on ethical, still less legal grounds.

Thucydides' Melian dialogue in fact provides a neat illustration of this point. The Athenian argument here can be summarised as 'might is right': in other words, the Athenians have the military resources to subjugate the Melians, so the Melians had better give in. They therefore conduct the debate in terms of what is most advantageous for both parties: for the Athenians to add to their empire; for the Melians to avoid annihilation.[140] The Melians try briefly to change the terms of debate from what is advantageous to what is just – a position more familiar to modern international law (Thucydides 5.90). It is interesting how brief and half-hearted this attempt is. We do not know whether the Melians actually made this point; that Thucydides includes it shows that an argument for national self-determination was possible to make but difficult to sustain.[141]

The second, connected point is that the Greeks did not know modern conventions of behaviour in war. They did have conventions of their own, but they were observed differently and governed by different rules. The idea of a war crime was unknown in the ancient world. On the other hand, there were rigorous standards of religious belief, to which warriors on different sides could be held, assuming that they believed in the same gods. For instance, oaths could be sworn on each side to return the war dead or to observe the terms of a peace treaty.

The behaviour of the Greeks in *Trojan Women* would therefore have seemed shocking to an ancient audience but not beyond the entitlement of victors. The only deed for which the Greeks will be punished by the gods is a crime against the gods: the treatment of Cassandra by Ajax. The particular political tone of the drama is achieved by forcing the audience to view events almost entirely from the point of view of the conquered. (This goes further than Aeschylus does in *Persians*, a play that also takes as its theme the aftermath of an allied Greek victory over a mighty eastern power: the Persians of the title lament at length, but the Greek victory does not threaten their personal freedom.) However, *Trojan Women* is not a drama of uninterrupted lamentation. The women can on occasion react with great emotion to events, but they are just as likely to offer a rational appraisal of their predicament. It is sometimes the very ordinariness of their manner, notwithstanding their royal status and a Euripidean ability to argue and debate, that invites sympathy in the face of great suffering.[142] At the heart of the action is Hecabe, who faces much of what is thrown at her with extraordinary dignity. When at one point she swoons and the chorus leader bids attendants to help her up, she says (462–73):

> No. Let me lie where I have fallen. Kind acts, my maids,
> Must be unkind, unwanted. All that I endure
> And have endured and shall, deserves to strike me down.
> O gods! What wretched things to call on – gods! – for help
> Although the decorous action is to invoke their aid
> When all our hands lay hold on is unhappiness.
> No. It is my pleasure first to tell good fortune's tale,
> To cast its count more sadly against disasters now.

She goes on to recount the reverses of her life and, in particular, the extent of her and Priam's tragedy in comparison with their previous great wealth and power.

As well as providing some reflection on the behaviour of victorious armies, *Trojan Women* also adds to our understanding of the domestic in political tragedy. In ch. 3 I suggested that female figures in tragedy become politicised when they intrude into the public life of the *polis*. In *Trojan Women* almost the opposite happens: the world of war intrudes into the lives of females. The *oikos* of each woman is politicised in that it is broken apart by the violent acts of men. Hecabe's husband and all of her sons have been killed, as well as her daughter Polyxena. Cassandra remains unmarried (see the discussion of the *Oresteia* in ch. 2). Andromache has lost her husband Hector and during the play loses her son Astyanax. Helen, who provoked the war by leaving the *oikos* of her husband Menelaus to elope with Paris, has now lost Paris. (She refers also at 959–60 to a subsequent brief marriage with the Trojan Deiphobus, although these lines are probably a post-Euripidean addition.) Each of these women must leave for different Greek cities, deprived of their own families. As women they were already among the 'others', differentiated from men (see ch. 2); to this status we can now add their projected otherness as exiles and slaves.[143]

There are two ways in which this destruction of the *oikos* is underlined. The first concerns the previous social station of the women. To be taken across the sea to begin a new life as a slave is presented as an enormous upheaval if you have only known the domestic life of a respectable woman.[144] When at one point Hecabe uses a sailing metaphor (always good with an Athenian audience) to describe her emotions, we find out that she has never been on a ship or even seen one (686–7; this seems the more surprising as Troy was near the sea). In the same scene, Andromache makes a speech that includes a lengthy description of a respectable woman's life. Such speeches are not unknown in Euripides, but this one has an especially tragic edge (643–60):

> But I, who aimed the arrows of ambition high
> At honour, and made them good, see how far I fall,
> I, who in Hector's house worked out all custom that brings
> Discretion's name to women. Blame them or blame them not,
> There is one act that swings the scandalous speech their way
> Beyond all else: to leave the house and walk abroad.
> I longed to do it, but put the longing aside, and stayed
> Always within the enclosure of my own house and court.
> The witty speech some women cultivate I would
> Not practice, but kept my honest inward thought, and made
> My mind my only and sufficient teacher. I gave
> My lord's presence the tribute of hushed lips, and eyes
> Quietly downcast. I knew when my will must have its way
> Over his, knew also how to give my way to him in turn.
> Men learned of this; I was talked of in the Achaean camp,
> And reputation has destroyed me now. At the choice

Of women, Achilles' son picked me out from the rest, to be
His wife: a lordly house, yet I shall be a slave.

A woman's ambition, the reverse of a man's, should lead her to the
quietest life possible; that was the Greek ideal (Phaedra in Euripides'
second, surviving version of *Hippolytus* is especially committed
to it). Paradoxically, this has brought Andromache an unwelcome
fame.

The second way in which the destruction of the *oikos* is underlined is through the debasement of the institution of marriage.[145]
Cassandra, having famously rejected the advances of Apollo, will
never marry; yet she is taken by Agamemnon to be a second partner
in his home. When Cassandra first appears, she is carrying a torch
– a symbol of marriage – and appears in her madness to be celebrating the union. But Apollo gave her the gift of prophecy: she goes
on to celebrate the role she will have in the death of Agamemnon,
a moment of revenge for her father and brothers. Either way, she
appears to mock the institution of marriage. Far worse is Menelaus.
I remarked above that his triumphalism on first appearance strikes
a jarring note. The terms of his triumph jar still more (860–6):

O splendour of sunburst breaking forth this day, whereon
I lay my hands once more on Helen, my wife. And yet
It is not, so much as men think, for the woman's sake
I came to Troy, but against that guest proved treacherous,
Who like a robber carried the woman from my house.

The punishment of the Trojan for breaking the rules of guest-friendship is not so shocking here: it is a familiar theme from Aeschylus'
Agamemnon. What is surprising is that Menelaus shows no interest
at all in restoring the marriage over which the war began: we learn
next that he is giving serious consideration to having Helen killed.
This is in contrast with the account in book 4 of Homer's *Odyssey*,

where Menelaus and Helen are seen back at home in Sparta, happily married and celebrating the marriage of someone else.

Trojan Women therefore presents a very different idea of the political from the other dramas we have considered: simultaneously more international in its outlook and more preoccupied with the institutions of the *oikos*. Yet, in forcing its audience to consider the effects of war, it is an undeniably political play, whether or not the irresistible correspondence with Melos is meant. If Euripides does have a point to make about Melos, he does well not to make it too obviously – and this is not only for fear of censure from the Athenians for criticising them in front of foreigners: there are good dramatic reasons, too. One can use a piece of drama to press home a political point about the effects of war, but one risks denying the usual complexities of a piece of drama for the sake of a single, rather obvious message. Euripides' drama is more subtle and for this reason more effective.

Some conclusions

These four plays take us through several levels of political inquiry, from what might be called the micro-political (how should citizens behave towards citizens?) to the macro-political (how should cities behave towards cities?). In between, we have been forced to consider questions of government in terms both of substance (best constitution) and of style (best leadership). Running alongside these purely political discourses has been the parallel and inseparable discourse of the *oikos*.

Earlier in this book (in ch. 2) I questioned the 'democracy assumption'. This assumption can be stated thus: any Greek tragedy speaks most clearly and obviously to the problems of the Athenian democratic *polis*. I hope to have demonstrated that political tragedy tends to be more broadly relevant to the Greek city-state, whatever its constitution. That said, there are still political points to be taken home from a tragedy that may have meant more to the democrat than (for instance) to the oligarch. This can be said because a piece of drama can accommodate a multiplicity of views. This dramatic potential is increased (see ch. 3) by the useful vagueness afforded by tragedy's heroic setting – unless the poet decides deliberately, as Euripides does in *Suppliants*, to set limits on this vagueness.[146] In the analysis of many plays, therefore, relevance to the Athenian democracy can simultaneously be assumed and dismissed.

If we make this assumption, then the rule of Creon in *Antigone* asks questions of a 'city first' political ideology that may have been associated especially with Pericles. If we make the assumption in *Ajax*, then the identification of the chorus with sailors from Salamis may have drawn in the poorer Athenians in the audience, the very people who gained most from democracy. On the other hand, these sailors are hardly in power in this play; in fact they are desperate for the protection of their heroic leader. There is no need to make the democracy assumption in Euripides' *Suppliants*, where the importance of Athens is linked unambiguously with the democratic system; but that is rather unusual for tragedy. *Trojan Women* is a more interesting case. The city of Athens does not appear here in any connection with democracy; instead it is mentioned once, briefly, as a kind of tantalising glimpse of the sanctuary that these women are being denied (we saw in ch. 2 that Athens is most frequently characterised in tragedy as a reliable source of political asylum). Or the play offers a lesson to the Athenians who treated Melos so harshly. Or both.

We must also look at these plays from a broader perspective, to see what questions were of interest to the life of the Greek city-state. Such questions include: how should citizens behave to each other? What responsibilities do they have to their families? Should I always obey the law, even when it is wrong? What should we expect of our political leaders? How much authority should these leaders have? These last two questions would have had added significance for those audience members who had prominent political roles of their own.

One question in particular is posed by all four of these dramas: how should one treat one's enemies once they are dead? This question can be asked either about personal enemies, as in *Ajax*, or about people defeated in war, as in the other three plays. We might take these plays as collective evidence that it was an important question to the Greeks; if so, there was not widespread agreement on the answer.[147] There *was* general agreement that to lose a war was to lose one's entitlement to freedom: war prisoners were commonly enslaved even if they were not killed (see Aristotle, *Politics* 1255a5–7). But if there was similar agreement that victorious armies could act in any way they pleased (and the arguments of the Melians to the Athenians at the very least imply dissent), why do some tragedies make this such an issue? And why does one's sympathy so often seem to be directed towards the unburied? There appears to be a tension between the notion that victors could treat the defeated as they liked and the belief that the dead should be honoured by burial.

The treatment of dead enemies is at the heart of the crisis at the close of Homer's *Iliad*. Both ancient and modern scholarship is divided over this line of verse (Homer, *Iliad* 22.395):

And he planned shameful (*aeikea*) deeds for divine Hector.

Achilles then drags Hector's body from his chariot around the walls of Troy. Is this famous act 'shameful' in the sense that it brings shame on Hector, or in that Achilles should be ashamed of himself? The Greek word *aeikea* can bear either meaning.[148] We might expect the gods to provide clues to the morality of Achilles' actions, yet it is not until book 24 that any gods condemn him; this leads him to return Hector's body on King Priam's request.

The tragedies discussed in this chapter present the same sense of crisis over the treatment of the vanquished. It has been suggested that this reflects a gradual undermining of traditional values over the course of the Peloponnesian War.[149] Tragedy, even more than Homeric epic, is the ideal medium through which to negotiate crises: it is not shy of grisly detail; it provides a forum for several points of view and does not need to prescribe a right answer. While it is not always easy to see what the tragic poet was supposed to be 'teaching' his audience, we do get a sense of what he wanted them to think about. These presumably were issues of interest to the tragic audience; they may have been important political issues of the day.

CHAPTER 5

THE POLITICAL RECEPTION OF GREEK TRAGEDY

A political act

'Just how far will a leader go in order to save face and secure a military victory in the East?' This question was posed in the publicity material for a National Theatre production of Euripides' *Iphigenia at Aulis* in the summer of 2004 (in a translation by the late Don Taylor, directed by Katie Mitchell). The words are cleverly arranged to create a parallelism between King Agamemnon and Prime Minister Tony Blair. The one man took the desperate measure of sacrificing his own daughter in order to save face with his troops and sail to Troy; the other took his country to war in Iraq and later needed to save face when he was widely accused of having misled parliament and the public in order to do so.[150] That said, there was nothing in the production itself that directed the audience to think about Tony Blair or anyone else in contemporary politics.

This was in contrast with another production in London during the same summer – this time an adaptation, not a translation. *Cruel and Tender* was written by Martin Crimp after Sophocles' *Women of Trachis* and produced at the Young Vic. It took what is by most measures a far less political play than *Iphigenia at Aulis* and politicised it. On one persuasive reading of *Women of Trachis*, the hero Heracles has spent his life ridding the world of its savage elements and yet his 'civilizing energies cannot be confined within the tame domesticity of Deianeira [his wife]'s house'.[151] In Crimp's version, Heracles has been transformed into 'The General', a senior military figure who has spent his life fighting 'terror' (clearly reminiscent of George Bush's 'War on Terror'); his presence in the family home is equally hard to bear. An even stronger contrast can be drawn with Peter Sellars' 1993 production of Aeschylus' *Persians*: Robert Auletta's version translates not just Greek into English but also the scene from fifth-century Susa to Baghdad in 1991, where the Iraqis learn of their defeat at the hands of the Americans. It does not matter that the Persians have become Mesopotamians (the ancient Greeks themselves could confuse Persians with Medes). The point is that this *Persians* worked rather as the original of 472 BC must have done: Sellars, as an American, was taking an Iraqi perspective on a recent American victory.

The National Theatre *Iphigenia*'s relevance to the 2003 Iraq War was nothing like as pointed. Beyond the prompt of the publicity, members of the audience were left to watch a Greek tragedy and work out any political relevance for themselves. Did this diminish the political importance of the production? *Iphigenia* was presented in the same season as *Stuff Happens* by David Hare, that most political of modern British playwrights. Hare's play purports to reconstruct the failed diplomacy that led to the allied invasion of Iraq. Euripides' play (see ch. 3) dramatises the equally political deliberations of allied commanders before sailing to Troy. The political effect of this *Iphigenia* was (deliberately?) gained in the programming as much as the staging.

This leads to two observations of relevance to the present chapter. First, it is striking that the nearest thing there is in modern Britain to state-sponsored theatre made implied reference to *the* political issue of the day in order to draw crowds to see a Greek tragedy. Second, merely to stage a Greek tragedy can be a political act. This was just as true, of course, in ancient Athens, with important differences. The festival in which the tragedies were performed was among other things a celebration of Athens; the tragedies performed there asked important questions about Greek *polis*-culture in general but (we have seen) rarely presented Athens in an especially bad light. By contrast, there have been times in the modern era when to produce a Greek tragedy has been to defy the state. Perhaps the clearest example of this has been in Greece itself during the dictatorship of 1967–74, when many Greek tragedies were banned from performance.[152] Even the publicity for Katie Mitchell's *Iphigenia* was designed in some small way to threaten the political establishment. We have seen that, while tragic drama could ask questions of the shared values of the Greek *poleis*, it was far less likely to confront the state head-on: that ideal of political theatre is more typically encouraged in a modern, liberal democracy.[153]

This short chapter considers the political weight and importance of Greek tragedy on the modern stage and screen – which has at times been considerable. A new production of a tragedy can acquire a political meaning that it never had in the original, whether because of the performance itself or the context in which it is staged. My title is therefore deliberate: 'The political reception of tragedy', not 'The reception of political tragedy'. To do full justice to this huge topic is impossible here. Rather, I shall consider two of the plays that I discussed in the last chapter in just a few out of many modern stage and screen versions: Sophocles' *Antigone* and Euripides' *Trojan Women*. This discussion is also limited in terms of the period of the performances, roughly 1944 to the time of writing. I hope that this will not give an impression that tragedy was sent down intact from the fifth century BC to the twentieth AD and that nothing happened in between. The performance history of tragedy is much longer than that, of course, even if tragedy has not been performed continuously from antiquity.[154]

I shall be illustrating two very simple points. First, modern performances of Greek tragedy can (and frequently do) supply political readings that cannot be sustained in the context of ancient Greek theatre and society; but (secondly) this does not matter. To put it another way, Aeschylus knew nothing of Saddam Hussein; knowing this does not reduce the political impact of Peter Sellars' *Persians*. I do not mean to say that every version of a tragedy is equally valid – that seems meaningless. What I do mean is that, just as ancient tragedy must be understood in its own cultural context, so must modern productions be understood in theirs. The purposes of some modern productions require the text to be stretched or even changed if it is to take on new political relevance and still make dramatic sense. Thus Sophocles' Heracles becomes Martin Crimp's General. Ignorant that such distortion has occurred, the viewer may be led to hold misconceptions about Greek tragedy in its original context; but this will not lessen the dramatic and political effectiveness of the performance. As audience members, we should be aware both of the existence of political anachronism and of its effectiveness.

Antigone the freedom fighter

During his time on Robben Island, Nelson Mandela once played the role of Creon in a reading of Sophocles' *Antigone*. Mandela records the event in his memoirs and can join Demosthenes on the list of statesmen to have quoted Creon's opening speech of the play with approval. But Mandela is no admirer of Creon:

> His inflexibility and blindness ill become a leader, for a leader must temper justice with mercy. It was Antigone who symbol-

ized our struggle; she was, in her own way, a freedom fighter, for she defied the law on the ground that it was unjust.[155]

So Mandela probably would take no issue with my discussion of Creon's leadership in the previous chapter. With Antigone, on the other hand, he goes beyond a view that would have been recognised by Sophocles' original audience (hence, I suppose, the qualification: 'in her own way'). It is true that Antigone is one of the most principled characters in Greek literature: she defies conventional authority and gladly dies for what she believes is right. It is also true that the people of Thebes support her and not their king. However, as I argue in ch. 4, she remains ignorant of the breadth of the support she has. More to the point, it is not her purpose to undermine Creon's rule, still less to free the people of Thebes from tyranny (assuming that Creon *is* a tyrant – see again ch. 4). She just wants to bury her brother and to join her family in the underworld.

Two broad developments in the political values of the modern West have changed the way in which audiences understand the character of Antigone. The first, as we saw in the previous chapter, has to do with the individual and the state. Greek tragedy is frequently concerned with the individual's place within the state; however, the way in which society understands that relationship was not the same in classical Athens as it is now. A dominant strain in modern liberal thought is the need to protect the rights of the individual against the government; this idea would have meant less to an ancient Greek. We have seen that, even in the comparatively liberal city of Athens, Pericles could praise tolerance in private life and a healthy fear of the law in public affairs, both in the same breath (Thucydides 2.37, quoted above on page 96).

The second development is the rise of feminism. Sophocles' play provides us with two competing models of female behaviour: Ismene and Antigone. We should be in no doubt that Ismene would have presented the lesser challenge to an ancient Greek audience. In the prologue Ismene refuses to help her sister, not because she agrees with Creon (she doesn't), but because she thinks that a woman is too weak to defy political authority. Antigone, by contrast, has been called a 'bad' woman in Greek terms.[156] Certainly in classical Athenian terms she is *bad at being* a woman; some might go further and say that she is a woman who is bad, a danger to society. Any admiration for Antigone would have been held despite the fact that she is a woman, not because of it. To an enlightened modern audience, on the other hand, the very fact of her womanhood gives an extra political edge to her protest: not only does she do what is right in defiance of authority, but she breaks free of the limits placed on her gender by society. The Greeks would not have recognised the truth of this second statement, for they did not tend to see the position of women in their society as unjust in itself. Some Greek authors could empathise with a woman's lot – as for instance Euripides does in *Medea* (see page 51) – but that was not to protest against it.

A modern western audience is therefore unlikely to understand *Antigone* in the same way as an ancient audience did, however faithful the translation and staging might be to the original. Modern audiences warm to the plucky individual who stands up before the might of the state, as the Chinese student did before the tank in Tiananmen Square. Antigone seems completely to have overtaken Creon as the most political figure in the play, for all that the last third of the drama is about him and not her.

The twentieth-century history of *Antigone* as a kind of protest song probably begins with Walter Hasenclever's German version of 1917, the product of his own experience of the First World War; but it begins in earnest in World War Two. Just as the potential of Antigone to become a freedom fighter is irresistible, so Creon is easily transformed into a fascist dictator. Bertolt Brecht wrote his *Antigone des Sophokles* soon after the end of the Second World War, and it was first performed in 1948. The full title notwithstanding, Brecht makes some significant changes to his *Antigone*. Many of the lines of dialogue have come from Sophocles via the eighteenth-century German translation of Friedrich Hölderlin. Other lines have been changed and many of the long speeches and choruses are abridged. Brecht also adds material of his own: most significantly, a prologue, set in Berlin in 1945, in which the sisters discover the body of Polyneices. The rest of the play is set in ancient Thebes but can be read as an ancient allegory of this opening scenario.

Brecht makes his Creon a far more sinister figure than he is in Sophocles' version. Creon's actions in Sophocles are dreadful and cruel, but the audience can make an effort to understand him as a man and as a politician. In Brecht, Creon – still an interesting character – is much more the unreconstructed mad tyrant. Here, the war with Argos turns out to be an act of aggression begun by Creon himself. Eteocles and Polyneices were both soldiers in his army, fighting for the same side. Eteocles has died in battle and Polyneices, who deserted as a result, has been put to death by Creon. His body has been left exposed to the vultures; Antigone and Ismene react much as they respectively do in Sophocles. If Creon is partially redeemed by his change of mind in Sophocles, this never quite happens here. He does, as in Sophocles, show some remorse when he confronts Haemon in the cave (see line 1262 of Brecht's version). However, his motive for rescuing Antigone is less principled: he needs to get his son back on his side in order to face down possible revolution in the city (1176 ff.). The long epilogue of Sophocles, which allows us to sympathise with Creon's suffering, becomes one short speech in Brecht (1278–85). Creon, who is addressed as *mein Führer* by the guard (186), thus provides an even stronger political force against which to react than he does in Sophocles' play.

Accordingly, the character of Antigone is politicised to a far greater extent even than in Sophocles' original. Her first dialogue with Creon is extended and becomes a debate on the nature of Creon's rule.[157] More generally, she considers her own actions as much in political as personal terms. When Creon asks her why she is acting so stubbornly, she replies, 'To set an example' (line 390 of Brecht, in the English translation of Judith Malina). In Sophocles, Antigone's primary motive (loyalty to family) is personal, not political. She certainly does not consider that she will serve as an inspiration to others.

Brecht also makes more of the backdrop of war, in a way that suits a play set by proxy just before the fall of Berlin. In Sophocles, the war with Argos is over, a matter of celebration in the opening chorus; the rest of the play deals with the aftermath of war but not with war itself. In Brecht, the celebrations continue throughout most of the play – there are several references to the Bacchic revels that Creon has ordered. But there is a further way in which the war intrudes on later scenes. When Teiresias appears, his most important function is to reveal to the chorus what Creon appears to have been hiding: the war is far from over. In a messenger speech inserted by Brecht, the Thebans lose to the Argives, who press home their advantage by marching on Thebes (1119–63). As the play ends, the fall of Thebes is imminent. This event is not only contrary to every version of the myth but also highly unusual in real Greek tragedy, where (we saw in ch. 3) the city in which a play is set almost always survives. Brecht's extra half-scene – the extended first dialogue between Creon and Antigone – focuses largely on the conduct of the war. She asks when the young men of the city will return from battle (457), a question that the chorus will raise again following Teiresias' intervention (1097). She accuses Creon of turning her brother Eteocles into the butcher of Argos (411–18). She worries that a leader with an aggressive foreign policy might turn his aggression on his own people (431–4). And she questions Creon's motive in starting the war in the first place (438–41):

The men in power always threaten us with the fall of The
State.
It will fall by dissension, devoured by the invaders;
and so we give in to you, and give you our power, and bow
down.
And, because of this weakness, the city falls and is devoured by
the invaders.

Perhaps the most celebrated production of Brecht's *Antigone*
was given for several years from 1967 by The Living Theatre, an
American company working in Europe. The story of this *avant-garde*
production comes across as a microcosm of the 1960s peace movement and its spreading influence. The Living Theatre's co-director,
Judith Malina, began to translate Brecht's German into English
while in prison in New Jersey. Her theatre company was alleged to
be withholding taxes, but the charges were dropped and may have
had more to do with a recently performed play that had been critical
of the government and the US military. Malina's remarks in the
introduction to her translation are a celebration of the new politics
of *Antigone*:

> The Living Theatre performed *Antigone* over a period of 20
> years in 16 countries – and wherever we played it, it seemed
> to become the symbol of the struggle of that time and place
> – in bleeding Ireland, in Franco's Spain, in Poland a month
> before martial law was declared, clandestinely in Prague – the
> play is uncannily appropriate to every struggle for freedom, for
> personal liberty that Antigone demands for herself.[158]

While some productions and adaptations of *Antigone* invoke
specific instances of political oppression, still others have actually been produced under such regimes and even (like Malina's) in
opposition to them. A French version by Jean Anouilh, performed in

occupied Paris in 1944, was clearly designed to celebrate the French resistance movement. Apparently the authorities put up with this as Creon was portrayed in reasonable terms; the political line of the drama could therefore be taken either way. Other productions during the twentieth century took place not only under fascism and apartheid but also under communist dictatorship.[159]

A particularly interesting example from communist eastern Europe is *Antygona*, translated from Greek into Polish by Stanisław Hebanowski. It was produced by Andrzej Wajda in Krakow, in January 1984. This was a period of great civil unrest in Poland. Martial law had been imposed from 1981 to 1983 and the trade union, *Solidarność* ('Solidarity'), had been made illegal. The leader of *Solidarność*, Lech Wałesa, would later become president of Poland following the fall of the communist system; but his position at this stage was less secure. Awarded the Nobel Peace Prize in 1983, he had to accept *in absentia* for fear that he would not be allowed back into Poland. Wajda's production was political in every respect. With the programme came a booklet containing work by the Polish poet – and well-known protester – Czesław Miłosz, alongside a number of photographs. Most of these photographs show contemporary scenes of war and protest from around the world. Two appear to show Pope John Paul II comforting a frail old woman and a small child. One of the last images is of a smiling man holding a crucifix. Wałesa was a devout Catholic, and the Pope – himself Polish by birth – one of his greatest supporters. As one authority on Wajda's work puts it, 'Even before the play had begun a member of the audience, seated in his chair with the programme in his hand, would be in no doubt as to what the director and actors wished to convey to him'.[160] The chorus of *Antygona* appeared in various costumes: first as commandos, wearing helmets and carrying guns; later as shipyard workers, a clear reference to the origins of *Solidarność* in the ship-yards of Gdansk. The performance politicised its audience: 'Some people stood up and applauded loudly, others remained seated and clapped politely, whilst others just whistled'.[161] Such contrasting reactions were reflected in the reception *Antygona* received in the press.[162]

The modern political values that attract audiences to *Antigone* are present even in those productions that cannot in themselves be considered political acts. An example is the excellent BBC TV version of 1986, translated and directed by Don Taylor. The nature of Creon's rule is suggested to the viewer in the very opening shot: vast portraits of the new king are raised into view by black-suited guards to a soundtrack of grim chords, low in the brass. The set is reminiscent of the Nazi headquarters in some Second World War films – a marble-floored hall with sets of high double doors on three sides, an antique desk set on a platform – except that an imposing flight of steps rises from the middle to a fourth set of doors. Antigone (played by Juliet Stevenson) enters this half-lit scene; first, however, she is seen walking against a background of white, as if to make a simple point about the 'good guys' and 'bad guys'. As she speaks to Ismene, she twice breaks off to look around her. As in the original Greek (lines 18–19), she mentions the 'risk of being overheard', but her anxious glances in this context seem to suggest the suspicious nature of a police state.

Creon (played by John Shrapnel) enters in the next scene through the doors at the top of the steps (more brassy chords, and a clash of cymbals) and descends to address the chorus from behind his desk. His dress, a white uniform with high collar and a cloak that he later discards, seems to suggest a dictator of some kind. It does not seem to matter *which* kind: a TV reviewer soon after the first screening remarked, somewhat vaguely, that 'John Shrapnel's bullet-headed martinet could have been one of the dour dictators the Russians installed in east Europe in 1945'.[163] Creon's language also keeps the political context usefully vague: the elders are 'Senators'; 'The fatherland is everything to us'; he talks of 'service to the Commonwealth'. It *does* matter that Creon appears fierce, even crazed, from the outset. He claims 'absolute power'. He rails against 'dissidents and subversive elements' (Taylor's translation of Sophocles, *Antigone* 219; the Greek means merely 'disobedient people').

Taylor's TV production is a nicely balanced piece of drama, and Shrapnel's performance is both commanding and moving. That said, the cumulative effect of what we might call the liberal tradition in modern versions of *Antigone* has been to upset the equilibrium of Sophocles' original. By setting her against a fearsome and unsympathetic dictator, writers and directors have been able to promote Antigone as a political heroine for their times; but occasionally something is lost in the portrayal of Creon. This has even been the effect, arguably, in a version not to have cast Creon as an autocrat. In Tom Paulin's *The Riot Act* (1984) the bombastic tyrant is replaced with the smooth-talking politician of a modern democracy. Paulin brings this out neatly by putting Creon's first speech in prose, while most of the rest of the drama is verse.[164] For all its effectiveness, Paulin's Creon has attracted criticism:

> The parody reduces Creon's authority and his position as a valid counterbalance to Antigone. In Paulin's play, right is expressed in Antigone's words. The dialectic of Antigone's right (personal, familial) confronting Creon's right (social, political) – which Hegel and others have noticed in Sophocles' play – is destroyed by reducing Creon to a cardboard politician.[165]

The same effect can be gained by reducing him to a cardboard dictator.

I have deliberately focussed on this liberal tradition, but there is plenty of room for other modern interpretations of *Antigone*, reflecting other political views and assumptions.[166] Recent productions have been set in some of the most politically volatile regions of the world: in the former Yugoslavia and among the Palestinians.[167] And perhaps the liberal consensus that has fed so many productions of *Antigone* is beginning to crack. Since September 2001 American and British politicians have felt able to defend some quite Draconian practices – most obviously imprisonment without trial – in terms of the security of the state. It remains to be seen whether future productions of *Antigone* reinstate Creon as the defender of these practices or come out all the more strongly in defence of personal freedom.

Trojan Women as an anti-war play

The theme of political protest continues with Euripides' *Trojan Women*. At the beginning of Michael Cacoyannis' film of the play (1971, with Katharine Hepburn as Hecabe), the following words scroll down the screen:

> In 416 BC, the Athenian army, engaged in a long and hopeless war, massacred the civilian population of the island of Melos in senseless reprisal. This incident drove Euripides to write the *Trojan Women*. Against the background of the sacking of Troy by the Greeks, he created a timeless indictment of the horror and futility of all wars.

We can ignore the historical liberties that are taken here (the women and children were not killed but enslaved; the war was not hopeless all the time and was officially not going on at all in 416/5). We may or may not assume that these events inspired Euripides' play (see ch. 4 on this question). What is more interesting to the present chapter is the last sentence, or rather the second half of it. It is always interesting to hear Greek literature described as 'timeless', as if it never had a time and a specific cultural context of its own. In fact, as I argued in the previous chapter, it is hard to believe that an ancient Greek could condemn war in such absolute terms.

To say that one is 'anti-war' in modern English would appear to mean one of two things. It could mean that, like Cacoyannis' Euripides, one has a principled objection to all wars; but few people are such complete pacifists. It can also mean that one is opposed to the prosecution of a particular conflict. This again is a comparatively modern phenomenon. Some anti-war protests in the modern era have become mass movements, like the one against the Vietnam War in 1960s America, or as the protest against the Iraq War briefly was in January and February 2003. *Trojan Women* in its first performance was not anti-war in either sense, although it did underline the plight of the victims of war; nevertheless, it provided natural dramatic material for anti-war protests throughout the twentieth century. This tradition has continued into the twenty-first century. An Australian production in early 2003, in anticipation of the coming invasion of Iraq, was set eighteen months into the future on the Persian Gulf. In the publicity material for the play, its producers set out their agenda unambiguously:

> [This production] is an unashamed protest against the impending US-led war in the Middle East. In this controversial production, Troy is on the coast of the Persian Gulf, and the Greeks are the western allies.[168]

One particularly enterprising use of *Trojan Women* as a means of political protest comes in Tony Harrison's play, *The Common Chorus*. This play is situated at the women's peace camp outside the gates of RAF Greenham Common. This base was used by the United States Air Force at various points in the second half of the twentieth century, and it was here in the 1980s that nuclear-armed Cruise missiles were deployed. In Harrison's play the female protesters put on two Greek plays for the benefit of the British guards. These guards' usual function appears to have been to yell obscenities at the women, while American voices can occasionally be heard through the crackle of the guards' walkie-talkies. The first Greek play is Aristophanes' *Lysistrata*. In this comedy, first produced in 411 BC, the women of the Greek cities refuse to have sexual relations with their husbands until the Athenians and Spartans make peace. Fantastically, this plan works and the play ends with peace talks between the two cities.

The second play is *Trojan Women*. The guards now take parts themselves, first as the gods in the prologue, and later as the Greek men, Talthybius and Menelaus. Much of this faithfully translates Euripides' original into English verse, but hints of the nuclear threat occasionally creep in. The following example corresponds to part of the chorus (lines 511–67 of Euripides) in which the women bewail Trojan foolishness in accepting the wooden horse (the capital letters are in Harrison's original):

They sang and they cheered, the people hurrayed.
They believed now the Greeks would never invade
and brought in this thing, and they were betrayed.
JUST AS WE ALL SAID HURRAY
TO THE WOODEN HORSE FROM THE USA.

The threat of nuclear annihilation fits well with the fate of Troy in *Trojan Women*.[169] Both affect the civilian population including women and children; more to the point, both mean complete destruction and no escape. Harrison's translation of lines 1291–2 reads, 'That great city Troy's no longer Troy'. A central paradox of *The Common Chorus* is that it engages with the prospect of mass destruction by presenting a tragedy in which the climactic event is the death of one small boy (Astyanax). But the larger picture is also well drawn: the Greek play ends with the burning of Troy, while in the external drama a convoy of cruise missiles arrives at the base. For the most part, Harrison achieves his effect by placing the staging of a Greek play in a highly specific modern setting and then allowing the audience to observe, as and when they occur, the points of correspondence. Or he would have achieved this if the production had not been overtaken by events. The cold war ended, the US Air Force and the women left Greenham Common, and the National Theatre chose not to produce the play after all.[170]

Conclusion

This brief discussion has looked at two Greek tragedies that have been especially politicised in modern performance. For the most part I have concentrated on just one aspect: the politics of protest. This, however, is a strong tradition in the theatre of some modern countries and perhaps especially in modern versions of Greek tragedy. Although many performances have been less clearly political, one tends not to be surprised when a director with a political agenda stages a Greek tragedy.

If anything, this increases our understanding of the ancient Athenian tragic theatre, by showing us what it was not. Of the ways in which modern theatre can be political, some are not found in Greek tragedy: there is no political allegory and only a few plays reconstructed recent history; there is nothing to show the effect of political decisions on the lives of the poor; there are no clear examples of political dissent. (Interestingly, all of these can be features of fifth-century comedy.) There is, though, a more fundamental difference between the politics of ancient Greek tragedy and political theatre today; this has to do with the way in which drama engages with the state.

In *Prospect* magazine for September 2004 there was an essay by Michael Coveney, entitled 'Liberal Dramatics'. His argument (briefly) is that 'whereas the "political" once entailed counter-cultural dispute, it is now part of the mainstream'. Perhaps this reflects a 1960s notion of political theatre and the extent to which members of a 1960s counter-culture have themselves become assimilated into the establishment. Hence David Hare has become Sir David Hare and his plays – once fringe theatre – are performed at the National. But Hare's dramas are still designed to engage with recent events and even challenge the political establishment. (*The Absence of War*, produced first in 1993, reflects his dismay at the Conservative general election victory the year before; the political assumptions behind *The Permanent Way*, 2003, are critical of rail privatisation; and so on.) The 1960s generation of political dramatists may have grown up, yet it remains the case that, when one hears the phrase 'political theatre' in modern discourse, one is put in mind of political protest.

This was never really the case in ancient Athenian tragedy. Both modern political theatre of the liberal tradition and the ancient Greek tragic theatre can be described as political in the stronger of the two senses that I described in the introduction. In other words, the plays not only tell political stories but also have a function in the political life of the state. This, however, is where similarities of political function end. The political function of some modern plays is to provoke a radical response from the audience at least, to influence events at most, and in either case to set the drama against the political establishment. Fifth-century Athenian tragedy essentially *was* part of the establishment: the whole festival was publicly appointed and parts of it were publicly financed. In addition, for all the assumed heroic universe, tragic poets were wont to set their plays against the familiar landscape of the classical Greek *polis*; and they tended to treat cities and their citizens with a degree of respect. That the festival was controlled by the city does not mean that tragedy was part of the machinery of government; rather, it provided an opportunity, once or twice in the year, for political reflection. The ways in which tragedy and comedy fitted into this festival atmosphere were very different. Comic poets gained a licence to say things that were shameful or unspeakable at all other times, including ruthless satire against contemporary public figures. Tragedy was less well placed to offer criticism of individual politicians or policies. Nor was it easy for a tragic poet really to be critical of Athens. Instead, in many broader ways tragedy could ask political questions important to the life of the Greek city-state.

NOTES

Notes to Chapter 1

1. On Euripides' first and second versions of *Hippolytus*, see Peter Burian, 'Myth into *muthos*: the shaping of tragic plot', in P.E. Easterling (ed.) *The Cambridge Companion to Greek Tragedy* (Cambridge, 1997) pp. 178–208, at pp. 201–5.

2. See for example Malcolm Heath, *The Poetics of Greek Tragedy* (London, 1987) pp. 37–89, with a useful summary of his view on p. 88. The choice of title for the present book should not be understood to bring it into direct conflict with Heath's, which does consider political aspects of tragedy on pp. 64–71.

3. The word 'ideology' is subject to a number of competing definitions in the modern literature (see, for example, the discussion with further bibliography in Simon Goldhill, 'Civic ideology and the problem of difference: the politics of Aeschylean tragedy, once again', *Journal of Hellenic Studies* 120 (2000) pp. 34–56, at pp. 42–3). Where I use the words 'ideology' and 'ideological' in this book, I mean to suggest a set of values or beliefs that underpin a political system.

4. See for example Oddone Longo, 'The theater of the *polis*', in John J. Winkler and Froma I. Zeitlin (eds) *Nothing to Do with Dionysos? Athenian Drama in its Social Context* (Princeton, 1990) pp. 12–19, alongside the criticisms in Jasper Griffin, 'The social function of Attic tragedy', *Classical Quarterly* 48 (1998) pp. 39–61, at pp. 40–3.

5. For a recent survey of the populations of the Greek *poleis* (and for further bibliography) see John Bintliff, 'City-country relationships in the "normal *polis*"', in Ralph M. Rosen and Ineke Sluiter (eds) *City, Countryside the Spatial Organization of Value in Classical Antiquity* (Leiden, 2006) pp. 13–32.

6. See Simon Hornblower, 'Greece: the history of the classical period', in

John Boardman, Jasper Griffin and Oswyn Murray (eds) *The Oxford History of the Classical World: Greece and the Hellenistic World* (Oxford, 1986) pp. 118–49, at pp. 131–5.

7. The solid archaeological evidence comes from the fourth-century stone theatre built on the same site as the fifth-century wooden theatre. The lowest estimate for numbers in the fourth-century theatre is about 14,000. The radically smaller figure of 6,000 is based on the view that the fifth-century Theatre of Dionysus was not the large, semi-circular auditorium that it would later become but shared the more intimate, rectangular shape of some deme theatres: see most recently Hans Goette's appendix to Eric Csapo, 'The men who built the theatres: *theatropolai, theatronai,* and *arkhitektones*', in Peter Wilson (ed.) *The Greek Theatre and Festivals: Documentary Studies* (Oxford, 2007) pp. 116–21. For an introduction to the evidence (and ultimately a rejection of the rectangular hypothesis) see David Wiles, *Tragedy in Athens: Performance Space and Theatrical Meaning* (Cambridge, 1997) pp. 23 ff., especially pp. 51–2.

8. See Simon Goldhill, 'The audience of Athenian tragedy', in Easterling (note 1) pp. 54–68, at pp. 58–60. See also note 33 below.

9. Arguing that the ticket price limited attendance by poor citizens: Alan H. Sommerstein, 'The theatre audience, the *Demos*, and the *Suppliants* of Aeschylus', in Christopher Pelling (ed.) *Greek Tragedy and the Historian* (Oxford, 1997) pp. 63–79. He describes two obols thus (p. 66): 'a third of an oarsman's or a building worker's daily pay'. However, part of Sommerstein's argument here, that the price was raised at some point in the fifth century, has no firm basis in evidence. There is only slim evidence that the Theoric Fund existed in the fifth century (*pace* Goldhill (note 8) pp. 66–7). Plutarch, writing around the turn of the second century AD, reports a view that the fund was introduced by Pericles (and therefore before his death in 429 BC). More contemporary sources are suspiciously quiet about it: cf. P.J. Rhodes, *A Commentary on the Aristotelian Athenaion Politeia* (Oxford, 1981), p. 514, and D.M. Carter, 'Was Attic tragedy democratic?' *Polis* 21 (2004) pp. 1–15, at p. 5.

10. The principal evidence for the attendance of slaves (apart from Plato, *Gorgias* 502d-e, quoted on page 16) comes from the fourth century and is hard to take seriously on this point: Theophrastus, *Characters*

9.5, on the subject of the 'Sponging Man'. This man 'watches without paying his share, and the next day takes along his sons and their tutor [at his guests' expense]'. The addition of the tutor, a favoured family slave, may simply be a comic exaggeration.

11. J.J. Henderson, 'Women and the Athenian dramatic festivals', *Transactions of the American Philological Society* 121 (1991) pp. 133–47.

12. A.J. Podlecki, 'Could women attend the theatre in ancient Athens? a collection of testimonia', *Ancient World* 21 (1990) pp. 27–43.

13. The usual view of rigid seclusion between the sexes at Athens has been challenged by David Cohen in 'Seclusion, separation, and the status of women in classical Athens', *Greece & Rome* 36 (1989) pp. 3–15; or see his book *Law, Sexuality and Society: The Enforcement of Morals in Classical Athens* (Cambridge, 1991) at pp. 148–57. The situation can more plausibly be described in terms of separation: in other words, women could appear outside but were likely to keep themselves apart.

14. Goldhill (note 8), at pp. 62–6 does not think women attended; this appears to comply with his view (see ch. 2) of the festival as a part of the political machinery of democratic Athens that engaged a (male) citizen audience in its ceremonial and dramatic performances. Goldhill presents his view on women spectators in more detailed form in 'Representing democracy: women at the Great Dionysia', in Robin Osborne and Simon Hornblower (eds) *Ritual, Finance, Politics: Athenian Democratic Accounts Presented to David Lewis* (Oxford, 1994) pp. 347–69. Henderson (note 11) and Podlecki (note 12) argue that women could attend – persuasively, in my view. On the social position of Athenian women, see further ch. 3, with the select bibliography on p. 191.

15. Peter Wilson, 'Leading the tragic *khoros*', in Pelling (note 9) pp. 81–108, at p. 96.

Notes to Chapter 2

16. Some would disagree, perhaps especially Michael Vickers, who has looked for political allegory in many Greek tragedies. See for instance his reading of Sophocles' *Philoctetes* in 'Alcibiades on stage: *Philoctetes*

and *Cyclops*', *Historia* 36 (1987) pp. 171–97. He supplies a wealth of
detail from the text in order to identify Philoctetes with Alcibiades. It
is broadly true that if you look for something hard enough in a work
of literature you will find it. Hence those who look for political allegory in tragedy will find many details to support their case (alongside
many that do not), but this does not make their readings any more
authentic. Angus Bowie provides a more subtle reading of *Philoctetes*
with respect to the career of Alcibiades in 'Tragic filters for history:
Euripides' *Supplices* and Sophocles' *Philoctetes*', in Pelling (note 9)
pp. 39–62. B.M.W. Knox, in *Oedipus at Thebes: Sophocles' Tragic Hero
and his Time*, new edn. (New Haven, 1957) at pp. 53–106 gives an
enterprising but (in my view) unconvincing allegorical reading of
Sophocles' *Oedipus the King*, in which he identifies the hero with the
polis-tyrant that Athens was in the eyes of other Greeks.

17. It remains controversial whether comic poets enjoyed a special
    freedom from the Athenian laws against slander (arguing that
    they did: Stephen Halliwell, 'Comic satire and freedom of speech in
    classical Athens', *Journal of Hellenic Studies* 111 (1991) pp. 48–70;
    arguing that they did not: Alan H. Sommerstein, 'Comedy and the
    unspeakable', in D.L. Cairns (ed.) *Law, Rhetoric and Comedy in Classical
    Athens* (London/Swansea, 2004) pp. 205–22). However, it is clear
    that any attempts made in the fifth century to curb comic satire by
    legislation or the courts were either unsuccessful or short-lived: see
    Sommerstein, 'Harassing the satirist: the alleged attempts to pros-
    ecute Aristophanes', in Ineke Sluiter and Ralph M. Rosen (eds) *Free
    Speech in Classical Antiquity* (Leiden, 2004) pp. 145–74.

18. On these correspondences, see D.M. MacDowell, *Aristophanes and
    Athens: An Introduction to the Plays* (Oxford, 1995) pp. 85–8.

19. A.J. Podlecki, *The Political Background of Aeschylean Tragedy* (Bristol,
    1999) pp. 42–3.

20. Podlecki (note 19) p. 124.

21. See Alan H. Sommerstein, *Aeschylus: Eumenides* (Cambridge, 1989)
    pp. 25–32.

22. Plutarch, *Cimon* 8.7–9.

23. The marginal comment of a scholiast (ancient editor) on Aristophanes,
    Acharnians 504–6 tells us that that the allies brought the tribute to
    Athens at the City Dionysia. It seems from the fourth-century orator

Isocrates (*On The Peace* 82) that on at least one occasion in the fifth century money resulting from the tribute (it is unclear whether this means a surplus or the whole lot) was brought into the theatre at the Dionysia and displayed on stage.

24. We know from an inscription (*Inscriptiones Graecae* ii² 555) that crowns were proclaimed in the theatre from 305 BC. The literary evidence, which I discuss here, comes from two opposing speeches from a trial in 330 (Aeschines, *Against Ctesiphon* and Demosthenes, *On the Crown*).

25. Isocrates, *On the Peace* 82; Aeschines, *Against Ctesiphon* 154.

26. The first quotation is from Simon Goldhill, 'The Great Dionysia and civic ideology', in Winkler and Zeitlin (note 4) pp. 97–129, at p. 114; the second is from Goldhill (note 8) p. 54, his italics.

27. Goldhill, (note 26) p. 101.

28. Griffin (note 4) p. 47.

29. On how the programme of the festival might have fitted together, see A.W. Pickard-Cambridge, *The Dramatic Festivals of Athens*, 2nd edn. revised by John Gould and D.M. Lewis (Oxford, 1988) pp. 63–7.

30. Harvey Yunis, *Demosthenes: On the Crown* (Cambridge, 2001) p. 179.

31. For a detailed discussion of this problem, see William E. Gwatkin Jr, 'The legal arguments in Aeschines' *Against Ktesiphon* and Demosthenes' *On the Crown*', *Hesperia* 26 (1957) pp. 129–41, at pp. 135–41. On the possible legal shortcomings of Aeschines' case, see Chris Carey's introductory note in his translation of the speeches of Aeschines (Austin, 2000), at p. 160.

32. Goldhill (note 26) p. 104.

33. There is fourth-century evidence for *prohedriai* for foreign envoys at Aeschines, *Against Ctesiphon*, 76 and Demosthenes, *On the Crown* 28.

34. Lysias, *Funeral Oration* 7–11; Isocrates, *Panathenaicus* 168–74. See further Sophie Mills, *Theseus, Tragedy and the Athenian Empire* (Oxford, 1997) pp. 59 ff.

35. Cf. Heath (note 2) p. 65. On the following, cf. Carter (note 9) pp. 13–18, in which I ought to have mentioned the military assembly at Euripides, *Hecabe* 98–153.

36. The terms 'mass' and 'elite' are now very familiar to historians of classical Greece; their usefulness in distinguishing the top rung of

society from the rest outweighs their obvious imprecision. I use these terms here and elsewhere in this book along the same lines as Josiah Ober, in *Mass and Elite in Democratic Athens: Rhetoric, Ideology and the Power of the People* (Princeton, 1989). Ober (p. 11) describes several overlapping definitions of an Athenian 'elite'. The ones that interest me here are: (i) a wealth elite, comprised of men who had the huge funds needed to provide a *leitourgia*; (ii) a political elite, which was more-or-less a subset of the wealthy elite and included all the regular speakers in the assembly.

37. Mark Griffith, 'Brilliant dynasts: power and politics in the *Oresteia*', *Classical Antiquity* 14 (1985) pp. 62–129, at p. 73.

38. On the elite status of public speakers, see Ober, (note 36) pp. 112–18; and compare the discussion of Euripides' *Suppliants* in ch. 4 below.

39. Martin Revermann, 'The competence of theatre audiences in fifth- and fourth-century Athens', *Journal of Hellenic Studies* 126 (2006) pp. 99–124, at pp. 107–15.

40. Sophocles' *Oedipus at Colonus* is another apparent exception, although the chorus members have some local importance: see lines 145, 728, 831. For contrasting views on this problem see R.W.B. Burton, *The Chorus in Sophocles' Tragedies* (Oxford, 1980) p. 295 and C.P. Gardiner, *The Sophoclean Chorus* (Iowa City, 1987) p. 110; for an intelligent recent discussion, J.P. Wilson, *The Hero and the City: An Interpretation of Sophocles' Oedipus at Colonus* (Ann Arbor, 1998) pp. 108–16.

41. Scott Scullion, '"Nothing to do with Dionysus": tragedy miscon- ceived as ritual', *Classical Quarterly* 52 (2002) pp. 102–137, and (by the same author) 'Tragedy and religion: the problem of origins', in Justina Gregory (ed.) *A Companion to Greek Tragedy* (Oxford, 2005) pp. 23–37.

42. Mark Griffith, 'The King and Eye: the rule of the father in Greek tragedy', *Proceedings of the Cambridge Philological Society*, new series 44 (1998) pp. 20–84, at pp. 73–4; or see the introduction to his edition of Sophocles' *Antigone* (Cambridge, 1999) at pp. 56–7.

43. Richard Seaford, *Euripides: Bacchae* (Warminster, 1996) pp. 252–3.

44. Richard Seaford, *Reciprocity and Ritual: Homer and Tragedy in the Developing City-State* (Oxford, 1994) pp. 133, 136.

45. A useful summary of modern views on this problem is given by A.F. Garvie, *Sophocles: Ajax* (Warminster, 1998) pp. 184–6. On Seaford's

argument, see Jon Hesk, *Sophocles: Ajax* (London, 2003) pp. 86–9.

46. The view that Sophocles' *Ajax* is best explained in terms of hero-cult goes back to the introduction to Sir Richard Jebb's 1896 edition of the play (recently reissued: Bristol, 2004). Chief among what Seaford calls 'an accumulation' of evidence (in 'The social function of Attic tragedy: a response to Griffin', *Classical Quarterly* 50 (2000) pp. 30–44, at p. 37) is a scene in which Eurysaces is made to supplicate his father's body (lines 1171–81). It has been argued that this act foreshadows his later role as the recipient of cult: see A. Henrichs, 'The tomb of Aias and the prospect of hero cult in Sophocles', *Classical Antiquity* 12 (1993) pp. 165–80; cf. Peter Burian, 'Supplication and hero cult in Sophocles' *Ajax*', *Greek, Roman and Byzantine Studies* 13 (1972) pp. 151–6. But this act is (unusually) as much for the protection of the supplicated as the suppliant.

47. Erwin Rohde, *Psyche: The Cult of Souls and Belief in Immortality Among the Greeks* (New York, 1966, German orig. 1907) pp. 121–2, and Walter Burkert, *Greek Religion: Archaic and Classical* (Oxford, 1985, German orig. 1977) p. 206.

48. See Emily Kearns, *The Heroes of Attica* (London, 1989) pp. 141–2.

49. Seaford (note 44) p. 344.

50. Cf. Rainer Friedrich, 'Dionysos among the dons: the new ritualism in Richard Seaford's commentary on the *Bacchae*', *Arion* 7.3 (2000) pp. 115–52, at p. 141, and 'Don Quixote responds to the windmill: a riposte to Richard Seaford on the new ritualism', *Arion* 9.1 (2001) pp. 57–72, at pp. 63–5.

51. For a discussion of this problem, see Kearns (note 48) pp. 50–2, 208–9.

52. Cf. Griffin (note 4) p. 52.

53. Seaford (note 44) p. 276, and (note 46) p. 38.

54. See Philip Holt, 'The end of the *Trachiniai* and the fate of Heracles', *Journal of Hellenic Studies* 109 (1989) pp. 69–80, especially p. 74.

55. S.J. Harrison, 'Sophocles and the cult of Philoctetes', *Journal of Hellenic Studies* 109 (1989) pp. 173–5.

56. These views lie respectively behind two different editions of the play, by March (Warminster, 2001) and Kells (Cambridge, 1973).

57. For a more subtle and extensive analysis of the language of tyranny in Sophocles' *Oedipus the King*, see B.M.W. Knox, 'Why is Oedipus

called *tyrannos?*', *Classical Journal* 50 (1954) pp. 97–102, reprinted in *Word and Action: Essays on the Ancient Theater* (Baltimore, 1979), notwithstanding his unpersuasive conclusion, which equates Oedipus with Athens (on this view, see above, note 16).

58. This tension, between citizen actors and the 'others' that they often portray, is explained in somewhat sophisticated terms by Froma I. Zeitlin in 'Playing the other: theater, theatricality and the feminine in Greek drama', *Representations* 11 (1985) pp. 63–94, reprinted in Winkler and Zeitlin (note 4) and included in her book *Playing the Other: Gender and Society in Classical Greek Literature* (Chicago, 1996) as ch. 8. Part of Zeitlin's long and detailed argument is that tragedy tests 'masculine values'. She notes that various characters in tragedy are either men who adopt female roles or women who act like men; in a ritualist reading of her own, she emphasizes the Dionysiac element in this inversion of gender roles; another sense in which tragic figures 'play the other' lies in the act of tragic *mimesis* itself: male actors play the role of the woman, the barbarian, and so on. Zeitlin's essay meets with reasonable criticism in Griffin (note 4) pp. 45–6.

59. Simon Goldhill (note 3) at p. 50 points out that aristocratic inter-state relations of this kind may have been less frequent at Athens following the citizenship law of 451 (on which see page 71).

60. Simon Goldhill, *Reading Greek Tragedy* (Cambridge, 1986) p. 48; see his also useful discussion (pp. 48–50) of modern interpretations of this speech. On precisely what the citizens should fear in this passage, see page 96 below with note 95.

Notes to Chapter 3

61. Aristotle, *Politics* 1253a3. Cf. Paul Cartledge, *The Greeks: a Portrait of Self and Others*, new edn. (Oxford, 2002) p. 123.

62. Perhaps there was more than one citizen if the son had grown up and not left home, as in Aristophanes' *Wasps* or *Clouds*. On the extent to which sons of citizens inherited their fathers' houses when they reached the age of majority, see Barry S. Strauss, *Fathers and Sons in Athens: Ideology and Society in the Era of the Peloponnesian War* (London, 1993) pp. 66–72.

63. See for example John Gould, 'Law, custom and myth: aspects of

the social position of women in classical Athens', *Journal of Hellenic Studies* 100 (1980) pp. 38–59, at pp. 46–51, reprinted in his *Myth, Ritual, Memory and Exchange* (Oxford, 2001).

64. Cf. B.M.W. Knox, 'Sophocles and the *polis*', in *Fondation Hardt pour L'étude de L'antiquité Classique – Entretiens Tome 29: Sophocle* (1983) pp. 1–37, at pp. 7–9, although he perhaps overestimates the degree to which Euripides' *Electra* is political.

65. There are problems with the Greek text of *Iphigenia at Aulis*, which is clearly not all the work of Euripides. The work was first performed after his death and appears to have been finished by another poet. In addition, the text includes numerous interpolations by later actors and producers. However, the text at first performance recently established by David Kovacs (Cambridge Mass., 2002) is enough to support my conclusions here; see further his 'Toward a reconstruction of *Iphigenia Aulidensis*', *Journal of Hellenic Studies* 123 (2003) pp. 77–103. Whether or not *Iphigenia at Aulis* was all the work of Euripides at first performance, it was a political tragedy, the work of Greek poets, performed in front of an Athenian audience.

66. Kovacs (note 65) at pp. 87–8 considers Euripides, *Iphigenia at Aulis* 522–35 to be pointless and therefore spurious to the first performance. These lines are, on the other hand, considered to be 'probably by Euripides' by J. Diggle in volume 3 of his edition of Euripides (Oxford, 1994).

67. On these secondary characters in Sophocles, see D.M. Carter, 'The Co-operative Temper: a third dramatic role in Sophoclean tragedy', *Mnemosyne* 58 (2005) pp. 161–82. Mills (note 34) at p. 222 notes that the tragic Theseus normally appears in a supporting role.

68. On the qualifications for Spartan citizenship, see J.T. Hooker, *The Ancient Spartans* (London, 1980) pp. 116–18.

69. Cf. Euripides, *Hippolytus* 421–4 with D.M. Carter, 'Citizen attribute, negative right: a conceptual difference between ancient and modern ideas of freedom of speech', in Sluiter and Rosen (note 17) pp. 197–220, at p. 215.

70. The argument of this section appears in more detailed form in my paper, 'At home, round here, out there: the city and tragic space', in Rosen and Sluiter (note 5) pp. 138–72.

71. On some of following, cf. N.T. Croally, *Euripidean Polemic: the Trojan*

Women and the Function of Tragedy (Cambridge, 1994) pp. 174–85.

72. This distinction is made well by Zeitlin (note 58).

73. On the date of the stage building, see Oliver Taplin, *The Stagecraft of Aeschylus* (Oxford, 1977) pp. 452–9. On Aeschylus' use of the stage building in the *Oresteia*, see Alan H. Sommerstein, *Aeschylean Tragedy* (Bari, 1996) pp. 217–41.

74. See for example Croally (note 71) p. 184.

75. Especially in the language used: see Carter (note 70) pp. 147–8 and n. 20.

76. It is not clear that even this death takes place in view of the audience. For a survey of the problem, see Garvie (note 45) pp. 203–4, alongside the response in Hesk (note 45) pp. 101–3.

77. On the shortcomings of this explanation, see Alan H. Sommerstein, 'Violence in Greek drama', *Ordia Prima* 3 (2004) pp. 41–56.

78. Of the modern scholars whose work I discuss in ch. 2, this observation is especially important to Griffith and to Seaford.

79. See Taplin (note 73) pp. 129 ff.

80. I include Sophocles' *Oedipus at Colonus*, where the chorus members appear to have some kind of local authority: see note 40 above.

81. I make this argument in slightly more detail elsewhere: on the general harmlessness of the *dêmos* in tragedy, cf. Carter (note 70) p. 141; on faction in Euripides' *Heracles*, see lines 252–7, 217–21 and 588–92 with Carter (note 9) pp. 22–3.

82. Cf. P.E. Easterling, 'City settings in Greek poetry', *Proceedings of the Classical Association* 86 (1989) pp. 5–17.

83. Cf. Victor Ehrenberg, *Sophocles and Pericles* (Oxford, 1954) pp. 105–12.

84. On the extent to which this rule is and is not observed in tragedy, see Gould (note 63) p. 40.

85. For a strenuous expression of the contrast between Thebes and Athens in tragedy, see Froma I. Zeitlin 'Thebes: theatre of self and society in Athenian drama', in J. Peter Euben (ed.) *Greek Tragedy and Political Theory* (Los Angeles, 1986) pp. 101–41, reprinted with revisions in Winkler and Zeitlin (note 4). Zeitlin's view is criticised sensibly by Easterling (note 82) at pp. 13–14.

86. My position here is a little less strong than I made it in Carter (note 9) p. 14 n. 47, where I argued (against A.J. Podlecki, '*Polis* and

monarch in early Attic tragedy', in Euben (note 85) pp. 76–100) that Pelasgus is constitutionally bound to go to the people.

87. P.E. Easterling, 'Constructing the heroic', in Pelling (note 9) pp. 21–38, at pp. 34–5, provides a more detailed discussion of the constitution of Athens in this play but nevertheless undervalues the certainty of the chorus' reply at line 67.

88. On this and other aspects of the Athenian laws against tyranny, see Martin Ostwald, 'The Athenian legislation against tyranny and subversion', *Transactions of the American Philological Association* 86 (1955) pp. 103–128, especially pp. 113–14.

Notes to Chapter 4

89. See Garvie (note 45) at pp. 6–8 for a good survey of the views offered on the date of *Ajax*. He concludes that 'nothing contradicts a date in the 440s, but ... certainty is impossible.'

90. Cf. Carter (note 70) pp. 162–4.

91. Sophocles, *Ajax* 201, 565. On the identity and role of the chorus in this play, see further Hesk (note 45) pp. 47–51.

92. Cf. Ps.-Xenophon, *Constitution of the Athenians* 1.2.

93. Cf. Garvie (note 45) pp. 9–11.

94. Cf. Garvie (note 45) pp. 216, 315.

95. Aeschylus, *Eumenides* 700; see the note in the commentary by Sommerstein (note 21).

96. It may perhaps help to consider Menelaus as a Spartan: see Garvie (note 45) pp. 223–4.

97. In the real Athenian army, it appears that the award of a prize after battle (an *aristeion*) was decided not by a popular vote but by the generals (see Plato, *Symposium* 220d-e, where the generals decide, although they are open to persuasion; cf. Plutarch *Alcibiades* 7). The generals probably voted among themselves (Herodotus 8.123; see further W.K. Pritchett, *The Greek State at War* Part II (Berkeley, 1974) pp. 276 ff.). By contrast, in Sophocles' *Ajax* (line 1136) the general Menelaus has not himself voted.

98. Cf. Knox (note 64) p. 13: 'The two kings do not even claim that the horrifying penalty is meant to be exemplary; they simply exult vindictively in their power over the lifeless corpse of the hero whom

they feared to cross when he was alive. The claims of the *polis* are advanced by unworthy spokesmen whose low and spiteful ranting enhances the dignity of that heroic corpse they wish to defile'.

99. The first to make this observation (albeit not in these terms) was probably H.D.F. Kitto in *Greek Tragedy: A Literary Study* (London, 1939) pp. 121–3, although he revised his position somewhat in *Form and Meaning in Drama: A Study of Six Greek Plays and of Hamlet* (London, 1956) pp. 184–5, and the original argument appears in watered-down form in the third edition of *Greek Tragedy* (London, 1961). On the use here of the words 'competitive' and 'cooperative', see B.M.W. Knox, 'The *Ajax* of Sophocles', *Harvard Studies in Classical Philology* 65 (1961) pp. 1–37, reprinted in *Word and Action: Essays on the Ancient Theater* (Baltimore, 1979), C. Meier, *The Political Art of Greek Tragedy* (Cambridge, 1993, German orig. 1988) pp. 181–3, and Carter (note 67); cf. Charles Segal, *Sophocles' Tragic World: Divinity, Nature, Society* (Cambridge Mass., 1995) pp. 16–25, especially 17 with n. 2.

100. See for example Goldhill (note 26) pp. 108–9.

101. Hans van Wees, 'The Homeric way of of war: the *Iliad* and the hoplite phalanx', Parts I and II, *Greece and Rome* 41 (1994) pp. 1–18, 131–155, see here pp. 9–14.

102. The usual view is that the Greek middle classes increased as a result of the rise of hoplite warfare. Van Wees (note 101) pp. 147–8 has challenged this view: it may even be the case that hoplite warfare developed as a result of the rise of the middle class. Van Wees further argues that the Homeric hero fights not singly but accompanied by a unit of lesser men, and that this may have reflected the reality of archaic warfare (pp. 4 ff.). Nevertheless, the effect of Homer's narrative is to glorify the deeds of an elite and suppress the actions of other men. The ideology and practice of hoplite warfare, by contrast, denied any decisive role to an individual.

103. On competitive values in the classical *polis*, see K.J. Dover, *Greek Popular Morality in the time of Plato and Aristotle* (Oxford, 1974) pp. 229–34.

104. Cf. Goldhill (note 3) pp. 50–1.

105. See, for example, Christina Elliot Sorum, ' Sophocles' *Ajax* in context', *Classical World* 79.6 (1986) pp. 361–77, and J.A.S. Evans, 'A reading

of Sophocles' *Ajax'*, *Quaderni Urbinati di Cultura Classica*' 38 (1991) pp. 69–85.

106. Sophocles, *Ajax* 1381, 1399 with Garvie (note 45) p. 15.

107. This is the view of several recent commentators on the play: Brown (Warminster, 1987) pp. 1–2, Griffith (Cambridge, 1999) p. 2, and Kamerbeek (Leiden, 1978) p. 36, who neatly considers Sophocles' generalship 'if not as a matter of *propter hoc*, then at least as one of *post hoc.*' For the opposite view, see Karl Reinhardt, *Sophocles* (Oxford, 1979; German orig. 1933) p. 240.

108. See R.C. Jebb, *Sophocles: Antigone*, new edn. (Bristol, 2003) p. 42. A relevant law from the fourth century is quoted at Ps.-Demosthenes 43.51.

109. See Griffith (note 107) 122.

110. On this point, see Dover (note 103) p. 157. I do not mean to say, however, that the Greeks were incapable of entertaining a concept of rights *at all*: see further Carter (note 69).

111. This principle is observed elsewhere in Greek literature: see Mary Whitlock Blundell, *Helping Friends and Harming Enemies: a Study in Sophocles and Greek Ethics* (Cambridge, 1989) p. 118, especially n. 46. On the comparison of Creon's ideas with Thucydides 2.60, see also Ehrenberg (note 83) p. 147.

112. See Martin Ostwald, 'Was there a concept of ἄγραφος νόμος in classical Greece?', in E.N. Lee et al. (eds) *Exegesis and Argument: Studies in Greek Philosophy Presented to Gregory Vlastos* (Assen, 1973) pp. 70–104.

113. Cf. A.J. Podlecki, 'Creon and Herodotus', *Transactions and Proceedings of the American Philological Association* 97 (1966) pp. 359–71, at p. 363.

114. See Podlecki (note 113) pp. 359–64 for a comprehensive demonstration of this point, although he perhaps overstates Creon's status as tyrant.

115. On hints of the tyrant in this speech alongside more moderate political language, see Carter (note 9) pp. 20–1.

116. This popular position probably owes something to the influential view of G.W.F. Hegel. For Hegel, tragedy is all about conflict between two equally justifiable points of view. *Antigone* is Hegel's favourite tragedy, since it fits this model nicely: see A. and H. Paolucci (eds)

Hegel on Tragedy (Westport, 1962) p. 325. On my view here, cf. Griffith (note 107) pp. 48–9, and Suzanne Saïd, 'Tragedy and politics' in Deborah Boedeker and Kurt A. Raaflaub (eds) *Democracy, Empire, and the Arts in Fifth-Century Athens* (Cambridge Mass., 1988) pp. 275–95, at pp. 287–9.

117. Xenophon, *Hellenica* 1.7.22, quoted and discussed in D.M. MacDowell, *The Law in Classical Athens* (London, 1978) pp. 176–9. On Athenian attitudes to non-burial, see Robert Parker, *Athenian Religion: a History* (Oxford, 1996) pp. 43–8.

118. For three different views on Creon as tyrant, see C.M. Bowra, *Sophoclean Tragedy* (Oxford, 1944) pp. 72–8, Ehrenberg (note 83) pp. 54–61, Podlecki (note 113).

119. Cf. Mills (note 34) pp. 106–7: the ability to respond to persuasion is a typically Athenian virtue; contrast the Thebans, who respond only to force.

120. See Mills (note 34) pp. 97–100.

121. Croally (note 71) p. 210 makes the first point; Mills (note 34) p. 97 n. 32 makes the second.

122. See M.I. Finley, 'Athenian Demagogues', *Past and Present* 21 (1962) pp. 3–24, reprinted in his *Studies in Ancient Society* (London, 1974).

123. See ch. 2. On the 'new' politicians, elite by wealth rather than birth, see Finley (note 122), W.R. Connor, *The New Politicians of Fifth-Century Athens* (Princeton, 1971).

124. On the rise of formal political theory in the late fifth century, see G.B. Kerferd, *The Sophistic Movement* (Cambridge, 1981) pp. 139–62.

125. J. Peter Euben argues that Greek political theory had its origins in the aftermath of the Battle of Salamis, in 'The Battle of Salamis and the origins of political theory', *Political Theory* 14 (1986) pp. 359–90.

126. See A.W. Gomme, 'The Old Oligarch', in *Athenian Studies: Presented to William Scott Ferguson* (Cambridge, Mass., 1940) pp. 211–224, reprinted in his *More Essays in Greek History and Literature*, ed. D.A. Campbell (Oxford, 1962). Simon Hornblower argues for a later date in 'The Old Oligarch (Pseudo-Xenophon's *Athenaion Politeia*) and Thucydides: a fourth-century date for the Old Oligarch?', in P. Flensted-Jensen, T.H. Nielsen and L. Rubenstein (eds) *Polis and Politics: Studies in Ancient Greek History* (Copenhagen, 2000) pp. 363–84.

127. On the ways in which this *agon* reflects the contemporary debate between democracy and oligarchy, see further Mills (note 34) pp. 120–1.

128. Ps.-Xenophon, *Constitution of the Athenians* 1.1–5; Aristotle, *Politics*, 1279b11–80a7.

129. These two words are most famously used for democracy in Herodotus, where they appear in Ionic form: *isonomiê* (3.80) and *isegoriê* (5.78, quoted above on pages 119–20).

130. See Strauss (note 62) pp. 6–7.

131. Arguing that Aristophanes did not favour democracy: Paul Cartledge, *Aristophanes and his Theatre of the Absurd* (Bristol, 1990); arguing that he was in favour of moderate democracy and therefore critical of the radical politicians of the late fifth century: G.E.M. de Ste. Croix, 'The Political Outlook of Aristophanes', in Erich Segal (ed.) *Oxford Readings in Aristophanes* (Oxford, 1996) pp. 42–64 (originally an appendix to his monumental *The Origins of the Peloponnesian War* (London, 1972)).

132. Cf. M.I. Finley, *Politics in the Ancient World* (Cambidge, 1983) pp. 60–1.

133. On Cleon's proposal not to offer peace in 425, see Thucydides 4.21–2. Thucydides, no fan of Cleon, suggests at 5.16 that he had been a major obstacle to peace.

134. On these and other aspects of the play's dramatic space, see Croally (note 71) pp. 192–4, 198–9.

135. See Shirley A. Barlow, *Euripides: Trojan Women* (Warminster, 1986) p. 220, who suggests that Talthybius' actions after the death of Astyanax (he goes out of his way to wash the body and prepare the ground for burial, so Hecabe does not have to) show some increase in sympathy in response to the women's suffering; but he is also just anxious to finish the job and get home. On this and other ambiguities in the character of Talthybius, see See K. Gilmartin, 'Talthybius in the *Trojan Women*', *American Journal of Philology* 91 (1970) pp. 213–22, especially pp. 216–18.

136. Cf. Croally (note 71) pp. 197.

137. For two different explanations of the way in which these lines look forward to the hoped-for success in Sicily, see H.D. Westlake, 'Euripides, *Troades* 205–229', *Mnemosyne* 6 (1953) pp. 181–91, at

pp. 182–3, and P.G. Maxwell-Stuart, 'The dramatic poets and the expedition to Sicily', *Historia* 22 (1973) pp. 397–404.

138. There is a dubious story that Alcibiades, having urged the Athenians to subjugate Melos, bought a Melian woman and had a son by her (Ps.-Andocides, *Against Alcibiades* 22). A.W. Gomme, A. Andrewes and K.J. Dover, in *A Historical Commentary on Thucydides, Vol. 4: Books 5.25–7* (Oxford, 1970) p. 190, find this 'the most indigestible error in the whole speech'. But it does at least show that the presence of Melian slaves in Athens between 415 and 405 was plausible to a Greek author, albeit one writing probably in the fourth century or later. On the date of the speech, see Michael Edwards, *Andocides* (Warminster, 1995) p. 136.

139. Cf. Jasper Griffin, *Homer on Life and Death* (Oxford, 1980) pp. 92–3.

140. To base an argument around what was advantageous (*sumpheron*) reflected a dominant strain in moral philosophy of Thucydides' day: see Kerferd (note 124) pp. 111–30.

141. Cf. Carter (note 69) p. 205.

142. Cf. Barlow (note 135) p. 31. On the women's effective use of words and argument, see Justina Gregory, *Euripides and the Instruction of the Athenians* (Ann Arbor, 1991) pp. 155–83.

143. Cf. Croally (note 71) pp. 98–100.

144. Cf. Croally (note 71) p. 199.

145. On the subversion of the institution and ritual of marriage in the play, see further Croally (note 71) pp. 73–4, 87–97.

146. On 'heroic vagueness', see P.E. Easterling (note 87).

147. Dover (note 103) at pp. 310–16 notes that Greek cities could not be held to the same moral standards as individuals.

148. For the former view, see Griffin (note 139) p. 85 n. 9. For a persuasive argument that Homer does express disgust at such acts, see Charles Segal, *The Theme of the Mutilation of the Corpse in the Iliad* (Leiden, 1971), especially p. 13.

149. Croally (note 71) pp. 120–22.

Notes to Chapter 5

150. For instance, 'Blair did lie to the British people over Iraq war, says Howard' (*Daily Telegraph*, 30th September 2004). The more measured

judgement of the Butler Report (2004: paragraph 464), specifically on the published intelligence dossier of September 2002, was that 'judgements in the dossier went to (though not beyond) the outer limits of the intelligence available. ... The Prime Minister's description ... of the picture painted by the Intelligence Services in the dossier as "extensive, detailed and authoritative" may have reinforced this impression.'

151. Charles Segal, *Sophocles' Tragic World: Divinity, Nature, Society* (Cambridge Mass., 1995) pp. 26–68. The quotation comes from p. 39.

152. See Edith Hall, 'Aeschylus, Race, Class and War in the 1990s', in Edith Hall et al. (eds) *Dionysus Since '69: Greek Tragedy at the Dawn of the Third Millennium* (Oxford, 2004) pp. 169–197, at pp. 172–3.

153. On this distinction, cf. Griffin (note 4) pp. 48–9, although he underestimates the potential of tragedy to ask the more general questions that I list in the conclusion to ch. 4.

154. On some of the reception history of tragedy up to the twentieth century, see now Edith Hall and Fiona Macintosh, *Greek Tragedy and the British Theatre, 1660–1914* (Oxford, 2005).

155. Nelson Mandela, *Long Walk to Freedom* (London, 1995) p. 451. On Demosthenes, see above, page 107. This performance of *Antigone* may have influenced the fictionalised performance of the play in Athol Fugard's The Island (1973), on which see Lona Hardwick, 'Greek drama and anti-colonialism: decolonising Classics', in Hall et al. (note 152) pp. 219–242, at pp. 238–9.

156. The most assertive statement of this view is probably Christiane Sourvinou-Inwood, 'Sophocles' Antigone as a "bad woman"', in F. Dieteren and E. Kloek (eds) *Writing Women into History* (Amsterdam, 1990) pp. 11–38; cf. her 'Assumptions and creation of meaning: reading Sophocles' *Antigone*', *Journal of Hellenic Studies* 109 (1989) pp. 134–48, especially pp. 139–41. Her view meets criticism in Helene P. Foley, 'Tragedy and democratic ideology: the case of Sophocles' *Antigone*', in Barbara Goff (ed.) *History, Tragedy, Theory: Dialogues on Athenian Drama* (Austin, 1995) pp. 131–50.

157. Brecht, *Antigone des Sophokles* 407–86. See below on this debate. These lines are inserted, roughly speaking, just before line 521 of Sophocles's version.

158. Judith Malina, *Antigone, in a Version by Bertolt Brecht* (New York, 1984) p. vii.

159. Cf. Edith Hall 'Introduction', in Hall et al. (note 152) pp. 1–46, at pp. 18–19.

160. Maciej Karpinski, *The Theatre of Andrzej Wajda* (Cambridge, 1989, Polish orig. 1980) p. 103.

161. The review in *Polityka* 1984, no. 6, translated in Karpinski (note 160) p. 105. It should be noted that *Polityka* was a government publication.

162. See Karpinski (note 160) pp. 105–7.

163. Philp Purser, *Sunday Telegraph*, 21st September 1986.

164. Cf. Marianne McDonald, 'Classics as Celtic firebrand: Greek tragedy, Irish playwrights, and colonialism', in Eamonn Jordan (ed.) *Theatre Stuff: Critical Essays on Contemporary Irish Theatre* (Dublin, 2000) pp. 16–26, at p. 18.

165. McDonald (note 164) pp. 18–19.

166. Cf. T. Ziolkowski, 'The fragmented text: the classics and post-war European literature', *International Journal of the Classical Tradition* 6.4 (2000) pp. 549–62, at pp. 554–5.

167. See Hall (note 159) p. 18.

168. Publicity for *Women of Troy*, directed by Jenny Green and Robert Kennedy at the Belvoir St Theatre, Sydney, Australia in January and February 2003.

169. On other modern productions that have made this suggestion, see Hall (note 159) pp. 19–20.

170. The database of the Archive of Performances of Greek and Roman Drama (www.apgrd.ox.ac.uk/database) lists only one production of this play: at the University of Leeds sometime in the 1990s.

APPENDIX A

CHRONOLOGY

The Second Peloponnesian War (431–404 BC) is referred to here as three separate events: the Archidamean War, the Peace of Nicias and the Decelean War.

Date	Political events	Theatrical events
c.533		City Dionysia founded at Athens
508/7	Democratic reforms of Cleisthenes	
c.499		First production by Aeschylus
c.492		Phrynichus, *Capture of Miletus*
490	Athenians defeat Persians at Marathon	
484		First victory of Aeschylus at the Dionysia
480	Persians defeated at Salamis	
478	Foundation of the Delian League	
472		Aeschylus, *Persians*
c.471	Ostracism of Themistocles	
468		First victory of Sophocles at the Dionysia
467		Aeschylus, *Seven Against Thebes*
463?		Aeschylus, *Suppliants*
462/1	Reforms of Ephialtes; Argive alliance; ostracism of Cimon	
c.462?		Stage building built at Theatre of Dionysus in Athens
458		Aeschylus, *Oresteia*

456		Aeschylus dies in Sicily
455		First production by Euripides at the Dionysia
443	Ostracism of Thucydides son of Melesias: Pericles now unchallenged in Athens	
442?		Sophocles, *Antigone*
440s	Parthenon built on the Acropolis	
431	Start of Archidamean War with Sparta	
429	Death of Pericles	
426	Cleon attempts to prosecute Aristophanes	Aristophanes, *Babylonians*
425	Athenians under Cleon victorious at Pylos	Aristophanes, *Acharnians*
424		Aristophanes, *Knights*
late 420s		Euripides, *Suppliants*
421	Peace of Nicias	
416	Athenians sack Melos	
415	Sailing of the Sicilian expedition	Euripides, *Trojan Women*
413	Athenian fleet destroyed at Syracuse Start of Decelean War with Sparta	
411	Oligarchic revolution of the 400 at Athens	
410	Democracy restored at Athens	
409		Sophocles, *Philoctetes*
406		Deaths of Euripides and Sophocles
405		Aristophanes, *Frogs* Probable date of posthumous productions of Euripides, *Bacchae* and *Iphigenia at Aulis*
404	Athens defeated by Sparta; rule of the 30 tyrants	
403	Democracy restored at Athens	
401		Sophocles, *Oedipus at Colonus* produced posthumously

APPENDIX B

AUTHORS AND
SURVIVING WORKS

Works are given in probable order of first production. Dates where known are given in brackets.

Aeschylus (525/4–456/5 BC)
    Persians   (472)
    Seven against Thebes   (467)
    Suppliants   (463?)
    The *Oresteia*:   (458)
        the only complete trilogy to survive, consisting of:
        Agamemnon
        Libation Bearers (Choephoroi)
        Eumenides
Prometheus Bound (possibly not by Aeschylus)

Sophocles (c.496–406 BC)
    Ajax
    Antigone   (442?)
    Women of Trachis (Trachiniae)
    Oedipus the King (Oedipus Tyrannus)
    Electra
    Philoctetes   (409)
    Oedipus at Colonus   (produced posthumously)

Euripides (c.480–406 BC)

Alcestis	(438)
Medea	(431)
Children of Heracles (Heraclidae)	
Hippolytus	(428)
Andromache	
Hecuba	
Suppliants	
Electra	
Trojan Women (Troades)	
Heracles	
Iphigenia among the Taurians	
Helen	(412)
Ion	
Phoenician Women (Phoenissae)	(409)
Orestes	(408)
Cyclops (satyr play)	
Bacchae	(produced posthumously)
Iphigenia at Aulis	(produced posthumously)

Rhesus is included in the Euripidean corpus but is probably not by him and may belong to the fourth century.

Appendix C

Some heroic genealogy

The House of Atreus (royal family of Argos)

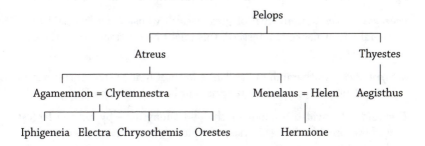

(Clytemnestra and Helen are the daughters of Tyndareus, from whom Menelaus takes over the throne of Sparta.)

The House of Laius (royal family of Thebes)

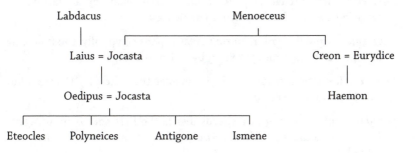

Appendix D

Glossary of Greek terms

Theatrical words

agôn – ('contest') a set-piece debate between two dramatic characters

chorêgos – private individual of great wealth whose *leitourgia* paid for a choral performance at a festival; this might be for tragedies at the City Dionysia

dithyrambos – (dithyramb in English) a form of lyric poetry, performed in competition by choruses of fifty men or boys at the City Dionysia

Dionysia – festival in honour of the god Dionysus – by far the largest was the Great or City Dionysia, of which the main component was the dramatic competitions

eisodoi – the two long side entrances to the performance space in the Theatre of Dionysus (sometimes referred to as *parodoi*)

episodos – a scene defined by a chorus at either end

exodos – the final scene of a tragedy

hamartia – Aristotelian term for a major error made by a character in tragedy (not, as often claimed, a 'tragic flaw')

leitourgia – a public work requiring great expense (typically, the financing of a chorus or warship) taken on by a rich individual

Lenaia – dramatic festival at Athens, smaller than the City Dionysia but also in honour of Dionysus

parodos – entrance song of a chorus, hence the first chorus in a tragedy (not to be confused with the *parabasis*, the chorus at the centre of a comedy) *prologos* – the first scene of a Greek tragedy, before the *parodos*

prohedria – (the priviledge of) a seat of honour in the theatre

stasimon – choral ode; the second chorus of a tragedy is the first *stasimon*

Political and other words

basileus – king, a hereditary monarch in contrast to a *tyrannos*; used especially of the king of Persia

boulê – the Athenian executive council of 500 citizens, elected annually by lot

dêmos – the citizen population of a Greek city; (as English 'deme':) an Athenian local government district

dêmokratia – democracy, the 'rule of the *dêmos*'

dikê – justice (notably in Aeschylus' *Oresteia*, on which see ch.2); also the word for a type of Athenian legal action

ekklêsia – assembly, in democratic Athens sovereign, open to all citizens and attended by up to 6,000 citizens every week or so

isêgoria – equality of opportunity to speak, especially in the Athenian *ekklêsia*

isonomia – equality under the law, used (especially early, and in Herodotus) as a synonym for *dêmokratia*

koinônia – community (see the beginning of ch. 3)

kurios – 'master': the term for an Athenian woman's legal guardian, whether her father, husband, brother, grown-up son or some other relative

metoikos – (in English, 'metic') a non-citizen permanently resident in Athens

nomos – custom, law

oikos – house, household

ostraka – potsherds, on which names were scratched as ballots for an ostracism (see ch. 1)

parrhêsia – ('saying everything') Athenian tendency to free speech

polis – city, city-state

politês – a citizen of a *polis*

sôphrosynê – moderate good sense, as not shown by some tragic heroes and therefore perhaps learnt by the theatre-goer

stasis – civil unrest, often associated in the seventh and sixth centuries with tyranny; in the Peloponnesian War with democratic-oligarchic struggles in some Athenian colonies

timê – honour, in the sense of respect shown to persons or institutions

tyrannis – Greek tyranny (defined in ch.1); defined as the bad form of monarchy by Aristotle in the fourth century

tyrannos – tyrant; generally used in contrast with *basileus*, but used with less precision in tragedy

FURTHER READING

Chapter 1

On Aristophanes' *Frogs*, see the introduction to the edition of the play by Alan H. Sommerstein (Warminster, 1997).

For two books written with the idea of poet as teacher very much in mind, see Justina Gregory, *Euripides and the Instruction of the Athenians* (Ann Arbor, 1991) and N.T. Croally, *Euripidean Polemic: the Trojan Women and the Function of Tragedy* (Cambridge, 1994). Both of these authors assume a stronger link between tragedy and democratic citizenship than I do. See now also Croally's chapter 'Tragedy's teaching' in *A Companion to Greek Tragedy*, ed. Justina Gregory (Oxford, 2005) pp. 55–70.

Several recent works can in different ways be described as 'audience studies' (in that they consider the nature of the audience and the ways in which it might have received the plays). See for example Alan H. Sommerstein, 'The theatre audience, the *Demos*, and the *Suppliants* of Aeschylus', in Christopher Pelling (ed.) *Greek Tragedy and the Historian* (Oxford, 1997) pp. 63–79, or Martin Revermann, 'The competence of theatre audiences in fifth- and fourth-century Athens', *Journal of Hellenic Studies* 126 (2006) pp. 99–124.

On Greek tyranny and its impact on fifth-century political ideology: James F. McGlew, *Tyranny and Political Culture in Ancient Greece* (Ithaca, 1993).

For a history of Greece during the period covered by this book, see J.K. Davies, *Democracy and Classical Greece*, 2nd edn. (London, 1993) or Simon Hornblower, *The Greek World, 479–323 BC* (London, 2002).

On the Athenian democracy, a useful brief guide is Chris Carey's *Democracy in Classical Athens* (Bristol, 2000). Among the many more detailed works, see especially M.I. Finley, 'Athenian Demagogues', *Past and Present* 21 (1962) pp. 3–24, reprinted in his *Studies in Ancient Society* (London, 1974), Martin Ostwald's *From Popular Sovereignty to the Sovereignty of Law: Law, Society and Politics in Fifth-Century Athens* (Berkeley, 1992), and Josiah Ober's *Mass and Elite in Democratic Athens: Rhetoric, Ideology and the Power of the People* (Princeton, 1989). On politics outside Athens, see the essays in Roger Brock and Stephen Hodkinson (eds) *Alternatives to Athens: Varieties of Political Organization and Community in Ancient Greece* (Oxford, 2000).

The best brief introduction to the Athenian theatre is now Alan H. Sommerstein's *Greek Drama and Dramatists* (London, 2002). *The Cambridge Companion to Greek Tragedy*, ed. P.E. Easterling (Cambridge, 1997) is an invaluable collection of recent essays. The following collections are also useful: Erich Segal (ed.) *Oxford Readings in Greek Tragedy*, (Oxford, 1983); Ian McAuslan and Peter Walcot (eds) *Greek Tragedy* (Oxford, 1993); M.S. Silk (ed.) *Tragedy and the Tragic: Greek Theatre and Beyond* (Oxford, 1996). *A Companion to Greek Tragedy*, ed. Justina Gregory (Oxford, 2005) is an impressive collection of essays that appeared too late to be of real benefit to the present book.

The classic study of the dramatic festivals is A.W. Pickard-Cambridge, *The Dramatic Festivals of Athens*, 2nd edn. revised by J.P.A. Gould and D.M. Lewis and reissued with supplement and corrections (Oxford, 1988). *The Context of Ancient Drama*, by E.G. Csapo and W.J. Slater (Ann Arbor, 1995) has an excellent collection of ancient sources in English translation.

On Aeschylus, see Alan H. Sommerstein, *Aeschylean Tragedy* (Bari, 1996) or Michael Gagarin, *Aeschylean Drama* (Berkeley, 1976). On all issues surrounding the authorship of *Prometheus Bound*, see Mark Griffith's *The Authenticity of Prometheus Bound* (Cambridge, 1977); he summarises the issues in the introduction to his edition of the play (Cambridge, 1983).

A great many good books have been written on Sophocles. Among the most distinctive in approach are B.M.W. Knox, *The Heroic Temper: Studies in Sophoclean Tragedy* (Berkeley, 1964) and Charles Segal, *Tragedy and Civilisation: an Interpretation of Sophocles* (Cambridge Mass., 1981). See also Segal's *Sophocles' Tragic World: Divinity, Nature, Society* (Cambridge Mass., 1995). Also recommended are G.H. Gellie, *Sophocles: A Reading* (Carlton, 1972) and R.P. Winnington-Ingram, *Sophocles: an Interpetation* (Cambridge, 1980). Mary Whitlock Blundell's *Helping Friends and Harming Enemies: a Study in Sophocles and Greek Ethics* (Cambridge, 1989) contains insights relevant to the study of tragic politics.

Euripides has not been quite as well served with general books. T.B.L. Webster, *The Tragedies of Euripides* (London, 1967) is still useful, especially in the ways in which he attempts to place the surviving plays in the context of Euripides' complete work. See also D.J. Conacher, *Euripidean Drama* (Toronto, 1967). For a brief introduction, see James Morwood, *The Plays of Euripides* (Bristol, 2002). Some classic essays are collected usefully in Judith Mossman (ed.) *Euripides* (Oxford, 2003).

Chapter 2

A.J. Podlecki's book has recently been reissued: *The Political Background of Aeschylean Tragedy* (Bristol, 1999). See also the introduction to his edition of Aeschylus' *Eumenides* (Warminster, 1989).

On the presence / absence of political invective, and other generic differences between tragedy and comedy, see Oliver Taplin, 'Fifth-century tragedy and comedy: a *synkrisis*', *Journal of Hellenic Studies* 106 (1986) pp. 163–74, reprinted in Erich Segal (ed.) *Oxford Readings in Aristophanes* (Oxford, 1996).

C.W. Macleod's article, 'Politics and the *Oresteia*' is in the *Journal of Hellenic Studies* 102 (1982) pp. 124–44, reprinted in his *Collected Essays*, ed. Oliver Taplin (Oxford, 1983). The first part of Macleod's article is a response to E.R. Dodds, 'Morals and Politics in the *Oresteia*', *Proceedings of the Cambridge Philological Society* 186 (1960) pp. 19–31, reprinted with revisions in his *The Ancient Concept of Progress and other Essays* (Oxford, 1973).

Simon Goldhill's article, 'The Great Dionysia and civic ideology' appeared originally in the *Journal of Hellenic Studies* 107 (1987) pp. 39–61. There is a revised version in *Nothing to Do with Dionysos? Athenian Drama in its Social Context*, ed. J.J. Winkler and Froma I. Zeitlin (Princeton, 1990). See also the relevant chapters of Goldhill's *Reading Greek Tragedy* (Cambridge, 1986). Goldhill replies to his critics (notably Jasper Griffin, on whom see below) in 'Civic ideology and the problem of difference: the politics of Aeschylean tragedy, once again', *Journal of Hellenic Studies* 120 (2000) pp. 34–56. Further criticism has come from P.J. Rhodes, 'Nothing to do with democracy: Athenian drama and the *polis*', *Journal of Hellenic Studies* 123 (2003) pp. 104–19, and D.M. Carter, 'Was Attic tragedy democratic?' *Polis* 21 (2004) pp. 1–25. On Goldhill's reading of Sophocles' *Philoctetes*, see Malcolm Heath, 'Sophocles' *Philoctetes*: a problem play?' in Jasper Griffith (ed.) *Sophocles Revisited* (Oxford, 1999) pp. 137–60.

For two different recent discussions of the relationship between tragedy and democracy see Suzanne Saïd, 'Tragedy and politics', in Deborah Boedeker and Kurt A. Raaflaub (eds) *Democracy, Empire, and the Arts in Fifth-Century Athens* (Cambridge Mass., 1988) pp. 275–95 (including an excellent brief survey of modern scholarship), and Jeffrey Henderson, 'Drama and democracy', in Loren J. Samons II (ed.) *The Cambridge Companion to the Age of Pericles* (Cambridge, 2007) pp. 179–95. Saïd makes what I call the 'democracy assumption' rather more easily than Henderson.

Mark Griffith's article, 'Brilliant dynasts: power and politics in the

Oresteia' is in *Classical Antiquity* 14 (1985) pp. 62–129. He develops his ideas further in 'The King and Eye: the rule of the father in Greek tragedy', *Proceedings of the Cambridge Philological Society*, new series 44 (1998) pp. 20–84. See also the introduction to his edition of Sophocles' *Antigone* (Cambridge, 1999).

On Athenian *chorêgoi*, see Peter Wilson, *The Athenian Institution of the Khoregia: the Chorus, the City, and the Stage* (Cambridge, 2000).

Richard Seaford's book is entitled *Reciprocity and Ritual: Homer and Tragedy in the Developing City-State* (Oxford, 1994). See also his commentary on Euripides' *Bacchae* (Warminster, 1996). Both Goldhill and Seaford come in for criticism in Jasper Griffin's 'The social function of Attic tragedy', *Classical Quarterly* 48 (1998) pp. 39–61 (see also his paper 'Sophocles and the democratic city', in Griffin (ed.) *Sophocles Revisited* (Oxford, 1999) pp. 73–94). Seaford responds in 'The social function of Attic tragedy: a response to Griffin', *Classical Quarterly* 50 (2000) pp. 30–44. The phrase 'new ritualism' was coined by Rainer Friedrich in 'Dionysos among the dons: the new ritualism in Richard Seaford's commentary on the *Bacchae*', *Arion* 7.3 (2000) pp. 115–52. Seaford replies in 'The Dionysiac don responds to Don Quixote: Rainer Friedrich on the new ritualism', *Arion* 8.2 (2000) pp. 74–98. The exchange concludes with Friedrich's 'Don Quixote responds to the windmill: a riposte to Richard Seaford on the new ritualism', *Arion* 9.1 (2001) pp. 57–72. A more comprehensive challenge to the various ritualist readings of tragedy has recently been made by Scott Scullion in his paper, '"Nothing to do with Dionysus": tragedy misconceived as ritual', *Classical Quarterly* 52 (2002) pp. 102–137, and see also his chapter, 'Tragedy and religion: the problem of origins', in Justina Gregory (ed.) *A Companion to Greek Tragedy* (Oxford, 2005) pp. 23–37.

For a whole book examining Greek society in terms of the 'other', see Paul Cartledge, *The Greeks: a Portrait of Self and Others*, new edn. (Oxford, 2002). Edith Hall's best-known work on the 'other' in tragedy is *Inventing the Barbarian: Greek Self-Definition Through Tragedy* (Oxford, 1989). See also her commentary on Aeschylus' *Persians* (Warminster, 1996). However, the views to which I refer here are found in Hall's 'The sociology of Greek tragedy', in P.E. Easterling (ed.) *The Cambridge Companion to Greek Tragedy* (Cambridge, 1997) pp. 93–126.

There are several other books that address, or partially address, political issues in Greek tragedy. One of the earliest and most influential is Jean-Pierre Vernant and Pierre Vidal-Naquet, *Myth and Tragedy in Ancient Greece* (New York, 1988, French orig. 1972 and 1986). Other books include: Christian Meier, *The Political Art of Greek Tragedy* (Cambridge, 1993,

German orig. 1998); J. Peter Euben, *The Tragedy of Political Theory: the Road not Taken* (Princeton, 1990). Collections of articles on the subject include: J. Peter Euben (ed.) *Greek Tragedy and Political Theory* (Los Angeles, 1986); J.J. Winkler and Froma I. Zeitlin (eds) *Nothing to Do with Dionysos? Athenian Drama in its Social Context* (Princeton, 1990); Alan H. Sommerstein et al. (eds) *Tragedy, Comedy and the Polis: Papers from the Greek Drama Conference, Nottingham 18–20 July 1990* (Bari, 1993); Barbara Goff (ed.) *History, Tragedy, Theory: Dialogues on Athenian Drama* (Austin, 1995); Christopher Pelling (ed.) *Greek Tragedy and the Historian* (Oxford, 1997).

Aeschylus' *Oresteia*: see introductory notes in the editions of *Choephori* [*Libation Bearers*] by A.F. Garvie (Oxford, 1986), and *Eumenides* by Alan H. Sommerstein (Cambridge, 1989) and A.J. Podlecki (Warminster, 1989). See also the general books on Aeschylus recommended above.

Chapter 3

Women in Athenian society: see (*inter alia*) John Gould, 'Law, custom and myth: aspects of the social position of women in classical Athens', *Journal of Hellenic Studies* 100 (1980) pp. 38–59, reprinted in his *Myth, Ritual, Memory and Exchange: Essays in Greek Literature and Culture* (Oxford 2001), or Roger Just, *Women in Athenian Law and Life* (London, 1989). On women in tragedy: Helene P. Foley, *Female Acts in Greek Tragedy* (Princeton, 2001).

On the use of dramatic space in tragedy: Oliver Taplin, *The Stagecraft of Aeschylus* (Oxford, 1977) and *Greek Tragedy in Action* (London, 1978); David Wiles, *Tragedy in Athens: Performance Space and Theatrical Meaning* (Cambridge, 1997); Rush Rehm, *The Play of Space: Spatial Transformation in Greek Tragedy* (Princeton, 2002).

The problem of finding contemporary political relevance for the Athenians in the heroic setting of tragedy is raised (with different but equally useful answers) by P.E. Easterling, 'Constructing the heroic', in Christopher Pelling (ed.) *Greek Tragedy and the Historian* (Oxford, 1997) pp. 21–38, and Mark Griffith, 'The King and Eye: the rule of the father in Greek tragedy', *Proceedings of the Cambridge Philological Society*, new series 44 (1998) pp. 20–84. This problem in essence lies behind a short but still influential essay by Jean-Pierre Vernant, entitled 'The historical moment of tragedy in Greece: some of the social and psychological conditions', which was originally published in French in 1972 and appears in English translation in Jean-Pierre Vernant and Pierre Vidal-Naquet, *Myth and Tragedy in Ancient Greece* (New York, 1988).

Chapter 4

Sophocles, *Ajax*: A.F. Garvie's edition of the play (Warminster, 1998), English and Greek with an introduction and commentary, is very useful. *Sophocles: Ajax* by Jon Hesk (London, 2003) is a detailed introduction to many of the major issues. On Odysseus as a co-operator figure in the play, see D.M. Carter, 'The Co-operative Temper: a third dramatic role in Sophoclean tragedy' *Mnemosyne* 58 (2005) pp. 161–82.

Sophocles, *Antigone*: there are editions of the play by A.L. Brown (Warminster, 1987) with English translation, and Mark Griffith (Cambridge, 1999); both have introductions and commentaries – Griffith's commentary is invaluable. On parallels between Creon and Pericles, see Victor Ehrenberg, *Sophocles and Pericles* (Oxford, 1954) – his approach seems very old-fashioned now but he tries hard to avoid the pitfalls of an allegorical reading (which I discuss in ch. 2). On my discussion of this play, compare the relevant chapter of Christian Meier, *The Political Art of Greek Tragedy* (Cambridge, 1993, German orig. 1988). On my discussions of both *Ajax* and *Antigone*, compare B.M.W. Knox, 'Sophocles and the *polis*', in *Fondation Hardt pour L'étude de L'antiquité Classique – Entretiens Tome 29: Sophocle* (1983) pp. 1–37 – a succinct discussion of all seven extant tragedies, following the motif of the obligations of the individual to his city.

Euripides, *Suppliants*: there is an edition in Greek with a commentary in a separate volume by Christopher Collard (Groningen, 1975). On the character of Theseus in this and other tragedies, see Sophie Mills, *Theseus, Tragedy and the Athenian Empire* (Oxford, 1997).

Euripides, *Trojan Women*: there is an edition in English and Greek with a useful introduction and commentary by Shirley A. Barlow (Warminster, 1986). Several political aspects of the play are discussed in N.T. Croally, *Euripidean Polemic: the Trojan Women and the Function of Tragedy* (Cambridge, 1994), although he arguably underplays the relevance of the Melian disaster.

Chapter 5

The reception of tragedy in recent years is considered, in greater depth than I can here, in *Dionysus Since '69: Greek Tragedy at the Dawn of the Third Millennium*, ed. Edith Hall, Fiona Macintosh and Amanda Wrigley (Oxford, 2004) – political aspects are discussed in a quartet of chapters by Oliver Taplin, Edith Hall (who discusses Peter Sellars' *Persians*), Pantelis Michelakis and Lorna Harwick, and see also the introduction to the volume by Edith Hall; a further chapter by Helene P. Foley considers various modern responses to gender politics in Greek tragedy. Also relevant are Marianne McDonald, *Ancient Sun, Modern Light: Greek Drama on the Modern Stage* (New York, 1992), and Fiona Macintosh, 'Tragedy in performance: nineteenth- and twentieth-century productions', in P.E. Easterling (ed.) *The Cambridge Companion to Greek Tragedy* (Cambridge, 1997) pp. 284–323.

On the modern tradition of *Antigone* in translation and performance, see George Steiner, *Antigones* (Oxford, 1984) – use his index to find what he has to say on versions by Hasenclever, Anouilh and Brecht. The versions of Sophocles and Brecht are compared (more usefully on the latter than the former) by Gisela Dibble, '*Antigone*: from Sophocles to Hölderlin and Brecht', in Karelisa V. Hartigan (ed.) .*Legacy of Thespis: Drama Past and Present*, Volume IV (Lanham, 1984) pp. 1–11.

Of the versions of Greek plays that I discuss, the following have been published in English: Robert Auletta, *The Persians* (Los Angeles, 1994); Jean Anouilh, *Antigone*, translated from the French with commentary and notes by Barbara Bray (London, 2001); *Antigone, in a Version by Bertolt Brecht*, translated from the German by Judith Malina (New York, 1984); Tom Paulin, *The Riot Act: A Version of Sophocles' Antigone* (London, 1985); Tony Harrison, *Plays Four* (London, 2002), which includes *The Common Chorus*.

All of these modern productions (and more) are on record at the database held by the Archive of Performances of Greek and Roman Drama, which is now available online: Amanda Wrigley (ed.) *APGRD Database*, www.apgrd.ox.ac.uk/database.

INDEX